IDYLLS AND RAMBLES

JAMES V. SCHALL, S.J.

Idylls and Rambles

Lighter Christian Essays

IGNATIUS PRESS   SAN FRANCISCO

Cover by Roxanne Mei Lum

The precepts of *Epicurus*, who teaches us to endure what the Laws of the Universe make necessary, may silence but not content us. The dictates of *Zeno*, who commands us to look with indifference on external things, may dispose us to conceal our sorrow, but not assuage it. Real alleviation of the loss of friends, and rational tranquility in the prospect of our own dissolution, can be received only from the promises of him in whose hands are life and death, and from the assurance of another and better state, in which all tears will be wiped from the eyes, and the whole soul be filled with joy. Philosophy may infuse stubbornness, but Religion only can give patience.

— Samuel Johnson, *The Idler*, Saturday, January 27, 1759

In the pictures of life I have never been so studious of novelty or surprise, as to depart wholly from all resemblance . . . Some enlargement may be allowed to declamation, and some exaggeration to burlesque; but as they deviate farther from reality, they become less useful, because their lessons will fail of application. The mind of the reader is carried away from the contemplation of his own manners; he finds in himself no likeness to the phantom before him; and though he laughs or rages, is not reformed. The[se] essays professedly serious, if I have been able to execute my intentions, will be found exactly conformable to the precepts of Christianity.

— Samuel Johnson, *The Rambler*, Final Number,
Saturday, March 14, 1752

CONTENTS

ACKNOWLEDGMENTS

All of the essays in this book were originally published in my column "Sense and Nonsense", in *Crisis* Magazine (1511 K Street NW, 525, Washington, D.C., 20005), except the following: Chapters 4, 5, 8, 10, 11, 15, 19, 26, 27, 29, 30, 34, 35, 37, 40, 42, 44, all of which appeared in *The Monitor*, the no longer published newspaper of the Archdiocese of San Francisco. Chapter 6 appeared in *The Catholic Standard* in Washington; Chapter 15 appeared in the *Georgetown Guardian*, a now defunct student magazine; Chapter 18 appeared in *The Academy*, a student newspaper at Georgetown University; Chapter 45 was a book review in *Crisis*, and Chapter 3 has not been published previously. The author wishes to thank these journals for use of essays included in this present book.

PREFACE

"DIGRESSING TO OUR HEARTS' CONTENT"

Of all the forms of literature, from epic drama to Aristotle's tightly reasoned philosophical lectures, from the novels of Jane Austen to the poetry of Dylan Thomas, the one I like best is the short essay. I have always loved the brief essay and have constantly, it seems, been writing one or another such essay all my life, even though the germ of my essay often began as a letter to someone. Indeed, collections of letters, as well as collections of essays, are also to me a joyous and wonderful part of our literature and of my habits of reading.[1]

Thus, given a choice, say, between the *Letters of Evelyn Waugh*, which a friend once gave me, or the *Habit of Being: The Letters of Flannery O'Connor*, which I bought down on Wisconsin Avenue in Georgetown, over against J. B. Morton's *Selected Essays of Hilaire Belloc*, which I have in two different editions; or W. E. Williams' marvelous collection in the Penguin series' *A Book of English Essays*, which contains one of my very favorite essays—which I like to read out loud—namely, Hazlitt's "On Going a Journey"; or Dorothy Sayers' *The Whimsical Christian*, which was originally entitled, in the English edition, *Christian Letters to a Post-Christian World*, I choose all at once. And so I find myself happily reading five or six books at the same time.

[1] See James V. Schall, S.J., "Letters and Spiritual Life", in *The Distinctiveness of Christianity* (San Francisco: Ignatius Press, 1982), 271–85; "The Recovery of Permanent Things: On the Christian Essay", in *Another Sort of Learning* (San Francisco: Ignatius Press, 1988), 169–86.

Thus looking at my desk and shelves, I see in various stages of being read or reread a pile of essays and near-essays, like letters and sermons and accounts. I see Walker Percy's *Lost in the Cosmos: The Last Self-Help Book*, the single volume Ignatius Press edition of John Henry Newman's *Parochial and Plain Sermons, Orestes Brownson: Selected Political Essays*, Madame de Sévigné's *Selected Letters*, Albert Camus' *Lyrical and Critical Essays, Meister Eckhart: The Essential Sermons, Commentaries, Treatises, and Defense, Boswell's Life of Johnson*, Marion Montgomery's *The Men I Have Chosen for Fathers* (one of whom, amusingly, is Flannery O'Connor). Next, I see Chesterton's *The Well and the Shallows* and, to go no further, *The Pickwick Papers*, which if not exactly a book of essays is surely close enough.

That list is a little chaotic, some sceptic will object, a little impossible also. Well, that is true, but anyone who understands the real wonder of the essay will comprehend what I say. Essays are indeed rather chaotic and not a little impossible. In his introduction to the Belloc essays, J. B. Morton caught much of what I have in mind. Belloc, of course, was one of the greatest essayists in the language, as was his friend G. K. Chesterton. Morton wrote: "The driving force of a good essay, that by which it lives and moves, is the character of its author. There are a hundred kinds of essay, because it is an intensely personal form of art, but whatever his method, the essayist discloses his own character."[2] The essay is suffused with the risk and the delight that constitute life itself, the one perhaps because of the other.

A book of essays is a wonder of different moods and humors, including, as here, a few essays that are sad. I know there exist those pedants who demand in their books subsections and unified themes. But those readers who demand these orderly things do not really enjoy a book of precisely essays, a book that can surprise and amuse and confound us at every turn of the page. In a book of essays, we find place for fancy,

[2] *Selected Essays of Hilaire Belloc*, with an introduction by J. B. Morton (London: Methuen, 1948), *v*.

for fate, for the flippant, for the fundamentals. We can talk of the universe or the corner drugstore, of God or the calf we saw on our cousin's farm, of something our friend told us about waiting or our critic told us about our weight. Likewise, in our essays, there is ample place for discussing our travels, places wherein we were happy or discontent. Too, in our essays, place is found for revealing our faith, place for our doubts, and place for what we do not know. Above all, there is room for wonder, for delight, for the excitement of discovery, and for our being simply astounded. We can talk in our essays of the death of our nephew and the loss of our eye, to see there some mystery we seek to fathom.

Morton continued of Belloc:

> Nobody could think that any one of these essays had been written by another hand. For there are certain recurring idio-syncracies, in addition to the more important ingredients of his style, which label the work as his. He will use contrast most effectively; a swift transition from wisdom to foolery, from uproarious fun to the pensive, the tender, the melancholy. And since one thing suggests not another, but fifty others, he will digress to his heart's content.[3]

What the good collection of essays presupposes, then, is the mystery of our being, its depths of joy and of how our sadness relates to it.

Essays reveal what it means to accomplish something and for whom. For ultimately we think we are given our lives to know the truth of things and to live with those who stand in this same world as we do. We want to live in the same real world with those we love. In such a world we can, indeed, *digress to our hearts' content* because *everything that is* falls under our gaze. The essay, unlike the treatise, does not neglect the little things in which everything takes its beginning.

Clearly, these present essays are touched by the spirit of Samuel Johnson, one of the most wondrous men in our litera-

[3] Ibid., *x*.

ture. *Idylls* and *Rambles*—these titles are from Johnson. These essays reflect too my own idylls and rambles. Here we find moments of reflective repose, walks, and travels that enable us to see our city and whether it is a lasting one.

Too I have added the sub-title, "Lighter Christian Essays", because I do not want to exclude the odd yet true Chestertonian notion that he who has the faith also has the fun. Of the faith of Belloc, which I share, Morton wrote that in Belloc's essays we find, because of this faith, "the old theme of the poets, the brevity of human life; beauty fugitive, joy transient, friendship and even love doomed to perish". These are solemn themes, to be sure, but who can deny that they are part of the life we live and on which we must touch if we are to reveal what we are, what we hold? The delight of the light essay is that it can touch as easily the sky or the cave; it can soar or be caught in the thickets because it can follow us wherever we go in our rambles and idylls on this earth.

In the passages from Samuel Johnson's *The Idler* and *The Rambler*, cited in the beginning of this collection, we see a certain seriousness about Johnson's project. He intended to suggest that the faith is an aspect in our seeing the whole, even though we should also know Epicurus or Zeno, and especially him whom Aquinas called "The Philosopher", that is, Aristotle. Johnson did not want us to miss the humor of our lot, as Boswell records for us again and again. Johnson himself certainly did not. But he warned us not to get too far from the stuff of the reality that we are, lest we not recognize ourselves in what is written.

Johnson, thus, wanted his suppositions to be Christian. That is, Johnson wanted the spirit that shone through what he wrote, whether idling or rambling, to assent to a definite view of the world which saw it as created, from nothing, but fallen somehow, as joyful yet tinged with the risk of evil, with the realization that we have a serious purpose.[4] Yet, he knew that joy too was itself the serious purpose of our existence. We

---

[4] See James V. Schall, *The Praise of 'Sons of Bitches': On the Worship of God by Fallen Men* (Slough, England: St. Paul Publications, 1978).

must allow our being lightness enough not to be oppressed but to be left free enough to laugh. We do this only if our vision of the world allows it. Our capacity to be amused depends in the final analysis on our philosophy, on how we see the world in its own reality.

In his essay "Christianity and Literature", C. S. Lewis wrote in 1939:

> The Christian knows from the outset that the salvation of a single soul is more important than the production or preservation of all the epics and tragedies in the world: and as for superiority, he knows that the vulgar since they include most of the poor probably include most of his superiors. He has no objection to comedies that merely amuse and tales that merely refresh; for he thinks like Thomas Aquinas, *ipsa ratio hoc habet ut quandoque rationis usus intercipatur* (reason itself insists that sometimes the use of reason be interrupted). We can play, as we can eat, to the glory of God. It thus may come about that Christian views on literature will strike the world as shallow and flippant; but the world must not misunderstand. When Christian work is done on a serious subject, there is no gravity and no sublimity it cannot attain.[5]

Such words, I think, capture the spirit of what I am about here.

In another essay from *The Rambler*, from Tuesday, April 3, 1750, Johnson wrote: "A French author has advanced this seeming paradox, that *very few men know how to take a walk*; and, indeed, it is true, that few know how to take a walk with a prospect of any other pleasure, than the same company would have afforded them at home." These essays, these lighter Christian essays, then, will be a kind of walk, a kind of adventure of the mind and spirit. In some ways, they are halting instructions on how to pray.[6]

We will find here places I have been, sometimes odd places, sometimes famous ones. We all have a context, and this is

---

[5] C. S. Lewis, "Christianity and Literature", in *Christian Reflections*, edited by Walter Hooper (Grand Rapids: Eerdmans, 1982), 10.

[6] See James V. Schall, *Unexpected Meditations Late in the XXth Century* (Chicago: Franciscan Herald Press, 1985).

mine, sometimes Rome, San Francisco, or Washington, lots of places in between. My friends, my family, my students, and many passing acquaintances are here in one way or another, for an essay, I think, is often occasioned by our friends and by those who pass us by.

Moreover, precisely fifty-four essays are found in this collection simply because that was the number of essays contained in Morton's collection of Belloc's wonderful essays. If there is some mystic reason for this number, I admit it.

What we read here, finally, contains the prospect of another kind of pleasure, that of the easy company of lighter essays. These essays need not be read all at once or in order. In these reflections, we can perhaps see new things, with their glimmer of that eternity in which our lives seem to be somehow engulfed, if we are to understand them aright. As they were for me, I hope also for the reader that they can indeed be idylls and rambles, that these essays can be light-hearted and Christian "efforts", attempts to catch briefly the permanence in our passingness, forgetting neither the one nor the other, because they both belong and are found deep in our unique lives.

I

No Point in the Happiness of Angels?

Before I left my room, I put a copy of Albert Camus' *Lyrical and Critical Essays*[1] in my black carrying sack with the red letters *The Tennessean* marked on it. I walked across the Potomac on Key Bridge—one of the world's loveliest vistas—to the Metro stop. The train came along shortly. On board, I took out the Camus, essays mostly from the early 1950s, and thumbed through it. I had already read most of the essays, even rereading "The Rains of New York" and "The Enigma" a couple of days previously. In fact, many of these touching essays have a special place in my heart. They describe cities I never saw around the Western Mediterranean—Palma, Oran, Tipasa, Constantine, Ibiza. I am always surprised when I miss something. More so, when I do not.

But as there was one essay that had no tell-tale marks of my pencil, I began to read it. It was called "Summer in Algiers". I got off the Metro to finish the essay while waiting at the bus stop. I kept thinking about it. Indeed, I wanted someone to read it to me, just so I would be sure it was as moving an essay as I had thought. Someone else's voice often makes things more real than our own silent reading of the same words.

What I remembered most was this sentence: "But I can see no point in the happiness of angels." I thought, how odd such a sentence is. Does Camus not know of Lucifer? The whole

[1] Albert Camus, *Lyrical and Critical Essays* (New York: Vintage, 1968).

point of angels, I thought, is precisely their happiness. In the most famous discussion about angels, not all angels chose happiness, some chose themselves. Saint Ignatius, in fact, almost as if the fate of the angels has something to do with us, asks us to consider their sin, not their happiness. But what did Camus mean exactly—no point to the happiness of angels? I tried to sort it out. I began to suspect that not only could he see no point to the happiness of angels, he could see no point to the happiness of men.

Another sentence thus riveted my attention. "In the Algerian summer I learn that only one thing is more tragic than suffering, and that is the life of a happy man." Happy angels have no point, while happy men are tragic. I have often maintained that joy is a greater mystery than suffering. We are much more hard pressed to explain our delights, to explain our splendor than to explain our pains and sufferings.

The account of Christ, no doubt, hints that suffering and joy can belong to the same life. Indeed, it suggests that suffering may be a way to joy. But the life of the angels does not involve suffering, though it does involve will, and hence good and evil. Christ had to become man to suffer. And he had to suffer because of will. Joy was his original lot. Joy is prior to suffering and hence its end.

I looked more carefully at Camus' theme. He was struck by the stark beauty of Algiers. He described the life there as intense, yet over quickly.

> People marry young. They start work very early, and exhaust the range of human experience in ten short years. A working man at thirty has already played all his cards. He waits for his end with his wife and children around him. His delights have been swift and merciless.

There is only life's living, its duty. Existence is without hope and therefore, so he wished to tell us, it is tinged with a kind of nobility, the only reward there is. Camus described the lives of the people he met. A sense of empty hopelessness pervaded his observations, but this was his thesis about all reality.

Camus wanted to think that any hint of hope or joy beyond its immediate living corrupted the experience of living itself. "For if there is a sin against life, it lies perhaps less in despairing of it than in hoping for another life and evading the implacable grandeur of the one we have." Here again is the classic sceptical thesis, one Camus shared with Marx, that somehow those who believe cause life to be less intense, less profound, less pleasurable, less attentive. The truth is pretty close to the opposite.

Plato, to this point, is our guide here. Diotima in the *Symposium* maintained that the experience of a single beautiful thing—every bit as existential as Camus could want—hinted at a beauty beyond itself in each thing's own beauty. Indeed, if it did not, the actual experience of beauty or joy would not be seen fully for what it is. Paradoxically, if the Christian experience is "unbelievable", it is not because it promises an eternal joy but because it wholeheartedly acknowledges a present one. The Incarnation is not designed to make joy less intense but more so. In Scripture the Incarnation is described in terms of nothing less than joy, great joy.

But what is it that Camus saw in his Algiers?

> Everything here can be seen with the naked eye, and is known the very moment it is enjoyed. The pleasures have no remedies and their joys remain without hope. What the land needs is clear-sighted souls, that is to say, those without consolation.

Camus sought to enhance the naked eye, the clear-sightedness. He sought to console by denying hope to joy.

Yet Camus remains a reductionist of sorts. It is not the pleasures or the sights or the joys themselves that are without hope. These remain what they are, realities whose very existence, whose mystery remains within them because they do not explain themselves. Deprived of their unavoidable tendencies to what is their source or origin or destiny, they do not remain themselves. What Camus described was pleasure or joy, minus the "bloom" (Aristotle's word) that made it pleasure or joy. Pleasure without hope is next to despair. Joy is most poignant when it is most joy. That we have here "no lasting city" was not intended to lessen our joys but to guarantee them as joys.

Camus wrote of his Algerians:

> One can find a certain moderation as well as a constant excess in the strained and violent faces of these people, in this summer sky emptied of tenderness, beneath which all truths can be told and on which no deceitful divinity has traced the signs of hope or of redemption. Beneath this sky and the faces turned toward it there is nothing on which to hang a mythology, a literature, an ethic, or a religion—only stones, flesh, stars, and those truths the hand can touch.

Aristotle said that man is a being composed of a mind and a hand. When man touches the stones, the flesh, and the stars, the truth that his hand touches is not merely the stones, the flesh, and the stars (though they are real enough), and what grounds him is something other than himself.

In the *Symposium* of Plato, we read, "The true order of going, or being led by another, to the things of love, is to begin from the beauties of earth."

"A working man at thirty has already played all his cards."

"I can see no point in the happiness of angels."

"Only one thing is more tragic than suffering, and that is the life of a happy man."

"If there is a sin against life it lies in hoping for another life."

"The pleasures have no remedies and their joys remain without hope."

We are more hard-pressed to explain our pleasures than our sorrows.

"The true order begins with the beauties of this earth."

The Incarnation is not designed to make joy less intense but more so. The point of angels is precisely their happiness, their choosing what is not themselves. Because he missed the point about the happiness of the good angels, Camus missed the point about the unhappiness of the fallen ones.

Our deepest joy is most poignant when it is most joy because it must be freely given and freely received. Without this there can be no happiness. That is the point, even for angels, even for ourselves.

2

In Pursuit of Nobody

This all started when I needed some sort of quotation suggesting that, lacking all else, civilization needed but two books, the Bible and Shakespeare. Searching my highly fallible memory, I vaguely recalled something that a young friend had written to me about a passage in A. N. Wilson's book on Hilaire Belloc.[1] I had in fact read the Wilson book, and according to my memory, this was the perfect quotation! I recalled it as reading: "In his last days, Belloc read nothing but the Bible, Shakespeare, and his own works." Naturally, nothing could have been more perfect for my purposes at the time.

I was next recounting this incident to another friend, who, it turned out, admired my memory but quietly hinted that there was something wrong with it. She was rather sure that this was not an accurate quotation except about Belloc's reading his own works.

So I finally resorted to the facts. The passage reads in Wilson as follows:

> Mr. Belloc himself . . . shuffled about between the study and the kitchen, and the chapel, and his bedroom. His reading now consisted entirely of *The Diary of a Nobody*, his own works, and the novels of P. G. Wodehouse, which he would read with the satisfied intentness of an old priest poring over his breviary.

[1] A. N. Wilson, *Hilaire Belloc* (Harmondsworth: Penguin, 1986).

About this time I thought that, well, perhaps civilization might just also be saved if instead of reading the Bible, Shakespeare, and Belloc's own works, it still read Wodehouse. But what was this *Diary of a Nobody*? How could that save civilization?

I had never heard of it. I went over to the reference desk of the Lauinger Library on our campus. I looked through the card catalogue, or perhaps the computer contraption that is now there to help you search for what should exist. I believe I finally found, in one of the early editions of the *Encyclopedia Britannica* under "Diary", a reference to this book and the name of the authors. They turned out to be two English brothers, George and Weedon Grossmith, who had originally published this book in *Punch*, in the 1890s.

George Grossmith evidently had something to do with Gilbert and Sullivan. Indeed, he turned out to be one of the original pillars of D'Oyly Carte opera company. George Grossmith was Jack Point in *Yeoman of the Guard* and the First Lord in *H. M. S. Pinafore*. Things were looking up. But our library did not have this book. I thought of trying inter-library loan, but by chance one of the reference librarians found that the book was still in print by Penguin.

So I hustled down to Olsson's Books and Records on Wisconsin Avenue. This was sometime last Summer. They did not have the book either but ordered it for me. Weeks passed, months. I went down every so often to inquire if it had arrived yet, as I was really curious to see the book. Finally, a very nice salesman told me, looking sadly at his computer, that the book was not available.

About two months ago, however, Scott Walter told me that he was on some sort of English booklist and noticed that *The Diary of a Nobody* was available. He asked me if I wanted it. I did. So for Easter Sunday I received an extremely handsome edition of *The Diary of a Nobody*, published in London in 1969 by the Folio Society, with an Introduction signed merely "J. H." and drawings by John Lawrence. I believe Weedon Grossmith did the original drawings.

Belloc is said to have thought this book "one of the half-dozen immortal achievements of our time" (originally published in 1892). This "J. H." more quietly says of it that it is "a minor masterpiece of unmalicious humour".

In the "Book World" of the *Washington Post* for April 2, 1989, moreover, there was a section on "Recommended Reading" that contained a brief notice by James M. Causey on, of all books, *The Diary of a Nobody*. Mr. Causey wrote: "Whenever you feel your life is mundane, when you think you hear twittering behind your back at the office or when you are treated rudely by a store clerk half your age, bring your problem to Mr. Charles Pooter (hero of the *Diary*). He has never let me down yet." The "twittering" settled it.

Several years ago I wrote a pamphlet for the Catholic Truth Society of London entitled *Journey through Lent*. The section on Holy Week was called "The Unsuccessful Man". I had forgotten about this until Scott reminded me of it and its source, which is, of course, from Belloc's poem "The Unsuccessful Man", which concludes:

> Prince, may I venture (since it's only you)
> To speak discreetly of The Crucifixion?
> He was extremely unsuccessful too. . . .

Now that I think of Belloc's love of this *Diary of a Nobody*, it seems that he saw in it a kind of Christ figure, of the fallible and failing man who somehow was the object of redemption. And it seems clear why Wodehouse would find himself in this same category. When Belloc read these books with the attention a priest should give to his breviary, perhaps he was engaged in a prayer for all those "nobodies" of which the world is mostly composed, including himself, his own works.

When I first recalled hearing of this passage in Wilson, when one friend told me of it, and another remembered it better than I, I was merely amused and delighted. But now I wonder if this amusement and delight did not portend that close connection of delight and sadness that Belloc understood so well, that is the very heart of the Incarnational world in which we live.

I will not recount the contents of *The Diary of a Nobody*. It is about the life of a man whose worldly affairs never quite go right, even though his is quite a good and normal life. The distance between his self-respect or dignity and how the world sees him is almost infinite. Life cures him of his illusions and therefore makes him the more poignant and in fact more decent.

On April 29, for example, Charles Pooter, a successful third-level businessman, has been having trouble with his son, Lupin. Lupin has at the time no decent job, is living at home, and has other—to his father—odd ideas. Pooter's wife, Carrie, is quite lovely but, maternally, she often has to side with the son. A couple of friends, Gowing and Cummings, come over as is their wont. Pooter, to liven things up, decides to tell them about his extraordinary dream. He had a dream of blocks of ice on fire, and it "was so supernatural that I woke up in a cold perspiration". Pooter was quite moved by his dream.

To this major event in his father's life, Lupin answered, "What rot!" Gowing added that "there was nothing so uninteresting as other people's dreams." Pooter appeals to Cummings, but he too had to admit that Pooter's "dream in particular was especially nonsensical".

Pooter replied, "It seemed so real to me." To this, Gowing retorted, "Yes, to *you*, perhaps, but not to *us*." And the *Diary* adds, "Whereupon they all roared." The reader cannot help but feel sorry for poor old Pooter, even though his dream was indeed boring.

During all of this, Carrie, Mrs. Pooter, was quiet, only to add finally to her husband's dismay, "He tells me his stupid dreams every morning nearly." Exasperated, Charles responded, "Very well, dear, I promise you I will never tell you or anybody else another dream of mine the longest day I live." At this good news, Lupin yelled, "'Hear! hear!' and helped himself to another glass of beer".

The subject was then dropped, and finally the Nobody's great dream and its recounting were forgotten when "Cummings read a most interesting article on the superiority of the bicycle to the horse." The Bible, Shakespeare, Wodehouse, Belloc's own works, and *The Diary of a Nobody*—these all are full of the Princes and the nobodies for whom The Unsuccessful Man lived and died.

3

Waltham Abbey

On a late Spring or early Summer day, there are few places on earth more beautiful than a green English countryside, or a walk along the Thames near Windsor or Maidenhead or Runnymede. Not too far away lies Waltham Abbey, built just a few years before Westminster Abbey, near the British Parliament itself. Waltham Abbey is one of those places which suddenly, when you encounter it for the first time, makes you realize again the tremendous complexity of our past. England was very old when Parliament was invented out of older, mostly monastic, traditions. This in itself, in turn, gives one considerable hesitation about predicting what any country's political future will be.

The ancient abbey is just north of London in the Essex countryside, along the Lea River Valley, the Lea Navigation Canal, not far from a very ancient forest. Waltham Abbey itself is Norman in style. The stonemasons who chipped the rock with axes for Waltham later went on to do the lovely Norman cathedral at Durham. The first impression of Waltham Abbey is a bit disconcerting, especially if you do not know its almost poignant history, as I did not when I first saw it on my last visit to England.

You expect, on first seeing it, something of the grandeur of St. Albans, Westminster, Bath, or Litchfield. But through a rather swaying, ramshackle passage, through an ancient pub (later to be checked for a pint of bitters), you pass through an aging graveyard surrounding an abbey structure that somehow looks quite incomplete or slapped together. The edifice seems to contain many levels of building construction, while the stone on the front tower, itself out of place, seems new and unblending.

Once inside, however, the abbey church is a stunning, neat, polished place. It is the local Anglican parish, which is in fact what saved the nave, for this is all that is left of a once greater, more vast structure. The rest was destroyed during the Reformation. What is left of Waltham Abbey, then, is but a shadow of its former glory. The place is associated with a miraculous "Black Cross" which was found in Somerset during the early Middle Ages. The oxen which were bearing the Cross to London refused to go beyond Waltham.

The Cross was set up right there, as a result. It is said to have healed King Harold, the last Saxon king of England. Harold thence proceeded to build the original abbey, completing it on Holy Cross Day, 1060. On his way to fight William near Hastings in 1066, Harold is said to have stopped to pray before the Cross, which sadly bowed its head, an ill omen.

Harold had failed to follow up his initial successes against William the Conqueror and was killed. He was so mutilated that it took his former mistress, one Elizabeth Swan's Neck, to identify the body. There are varying legends about what happened subsequently. One even maintains that Harold escaped and joined a monastery in Chester. But it seems that he was borne to Waltham to be buried underneath the main altar of the abbey church.

Waltham Abbey was greatly enlarged and turned over to the Augustinian monks by Henry II in expiation for his part in the murder of Thomas à Becket. Thus, the Abbey became one of the great monastic complexes in England. During the Reformation, however, the monks remained mostly loyal to the papacy, which turned out to be their death warrant under Henry VIII. Waltham was the last of the great monasteries to be secularized. The year was 1540.

The abbey was turned over or sold to the Denny family as a private estate. They destroyed the great church and buildings except for the nave and the central tower, which collapsed a few years later. The Lady Chapel of the abbey now bears a headless Madonna that was recently discovered in a nearby garden. Apparently, it was buried by the Catholics to save it from further destruction.

The abbey church's front wall was magnificently redone and filled in during the last century with exquisite stained glass windows by Edward Bourne-Jones. And as it is a Church of England establishment, there are now monuments to its founders, to the Denny family, to the soldiers of the many wars in which England has fought, to Robert Smith, a seventeenth-century merchantman.

Waltham Abbey is especially famous for its music and its bells. Thomas Tallis was organist here on the eve of the Reformation, when he became the father of English church music. The bells of the abbey were almost destroyed when the tower in the center collapsed. When the new front tower was built, the old bells were sold to pay for it. The present bells are famous as the "wild bells" in the almost messianic Canto CV of Tennyson's *In Memoriam.*

> Ring out wild bells to the wild sky,
>   The flying cloud, the frosty light:
>   The year is dying in the light;
> Ring out wild bells, and let him die . . .
>
> Ring out the old, ring in the new . . .
> Ring out the false, ring in the true . . .
> Ring in the Christ that is to be.

Yet, Waltham is not a messianic place. Rather it is the opposite, a place more of defeat and senseless destruction of a way of life and a tradition. The gravestone of Harold with the date, 1066, stands in eloquent testimony to an England that might have been, while the ruins of the front section of the abbey church and the surrounding cloister buildings remind us of how a religion was once changed.

On the beautiful canopied west door of the abbey church, there was hung a plaque with a sort of greeting prayer, sentimental no doubt, but worth saying still:

> Oh, God, make the door of this house wide enough to receive all who need human love and a heavenly Father's care, and narrow enough to shut out all envy and pride and hatred at its threshold, smooth enough to be no stumbling block to children or to starving feet, but rugged enough to turn back the Tempter's power.

No one knows today what happened to the Black Cross which disappeard when the monks were expelled during the Reformation. But it is, in this lovely ruined abbey, impossible not to wonder about it.

The sacristan who enthusiastically showed us through the lovely abbey told us cryptically that he was sure that "the Pope had it". With some effort, I suppressed the temptation, no doubt because of the prayer on the door, to tell him that if the Pope really had the English Black Cross of Waltham, we would surely know it. Anyhow, the sacristan said that they had written to the Pope twice already requesting the Cross, but it seems that he was too busy these days to answer the letter. Just the thought of some Vatican functionary puzzling through such a novel request is worth considerable amusement.

In a way, however, it would be right for Rome to have this famous Black Cross and stubbornly to keep it, since it was not safe in England in Harold's once lovely abbey. But it is undoubtedly not so that this Cross is somehow in Rome. Even "holy crosses" were lost during the Reformation. And while "wild bells" may "ring in the Christ that is to be", nonetheless, this warm, beautiful part of England recalls the sad King of the Saxons killed near Hastings in 1066.

The Holy and the Secular both are often defeated in this world. Waltham Abbey is to me this kind of a monument, a beautiful living ruins, a reminder of defeated things, wild bells that "call" not just to this life and its uncertain victories. The record of mankind is also one of defeat and loss. It is well to have such a lovely place in which to be reminded of this truth which is part of our human reality.

4

Last Days in Rome

Rome had become a familiar place to me during the twelve years (1965–77) I lived there, at least for a good part of each year, the Spring usually, to teach at the Gregorian University, near the center of the City. During part of this time (1968–77), I also spent the fall semester at the University of San Francisco, and I left both in 1978 to join the Government Faculty at Georgetown University in Washington. The following is my account, written as I left Rome, of my Last Days there.

So how does one leave this ancient, lovely place full of its own special noises and smells and colors? Our very culture has somehow made of Rome a place to which we bid a fond farewell because we cannot all live here, even though in a real way it is part of all of us. "Arrivederci Roma"—this song has become itself a reason for being so sentimental about this lovely City.

A city is great, I often think, according to the number of free things that are available in it. By this criterion, Rome is surely the loveliest and richest city in the world. A friend of mine had just co-authored a little book called *Rome for Children*, which, like any useful guide book as I look at it, seems like an endless list of things yet to be seen in this endless City.

I was talking to a Canadian lady at my friend's home one day, a lady who has lived in Rome for years. She told me that when she has visitors in town for a few days or a week, it is useless to tell them to go to visit this or that place. It is better to tell them just to go to a piazza, like the Navona or the Rotunda or Santa Maria in Trastevere, and just sit and watch. The most important thing is the atmosphere, the spirit of the place and the people in it. And this can come in no other way but just staying there for a time.

In the line of free things, the Roman churches often have surprising concerts. I do not believe there really is a good first-class high Mass in Rome on a Sunday. Sometimes, at St. Peter's, you can catch the Sistine Choir. San Anselmo's liturgy is good, for the most part.

There is, however, little real live musical presence in the Roman churches, unlike Vienna. But the other evening I went over to the Church of the Twelve Apostles, next door to where I live, to hear a concert of the Choir of the Cathedral of Uppsala in Sweden. In their blue gowns they were quite excellent—Bach, Gregorian chant, Swedish religious music.

Then a couple of days ago, the *A Capella* Choir of the University of Utah sang in the Basilica of San Lorenzo in Damaso. This was really an extraordinary choir of about sixty voices. Newell Weight was an outstanding director, superb really. Their sacred music was unforgettable. I especially loved their "Beautiful Savior" and "O Come, O Come, Emmanuel". It was justly appreciated and applauded. I thought, when Americans do things well, they do them especially well. I sometimes suspect our excellence is more of a problem than our failure, just as joy is more inexplicable than sorrow in its deepest meanings.

What Rome adds to the Cathedral Choir of Uppsala and the Choir of the University of Utah is precisely Rome—the setting where most of the sacred music is at home. Yet sacred music is not at home in a concert setting, even in the Dodici Apostoli or San Lorenzo, for it needs to have the solemnity of worship for it to be what it really is.

You should not applaud after sacred music, I think— something that an organist at the chapel at the old Lone Mountain College in San Francisco understood. Sacred music really should be part of a liturgical setting. Today in our religious services, I fear, we have worship without excellence in music, while our universities have excellence in music without worship.

So, on my last full day in Rome, I got up early to take a walk down back of the Imperial Fora. I chanced to cross a doorway I had never noticed before, over which was a plaque signed, "Rosavita, 1946".

The first part of this plaque stated in Italian: "Faith will accompany us." The second said: "From humanity, so many shadows; from God, so much light." It was a clear morning. The sun was just coming up. I walked to San Clemente with its great mosaics of the Lambs, on to San Giovanni in Laterano, with the sun shining almost directly into its main front doors, giving it much needed interior light, a lovely presence, mindful of our own abiding need of just this interior light. These ancient basilicas faced the sun by design, I recalled. The high priest always faced the people because of it. The heads of Peter and Paul are supposed to be encased here.

I stopped for a moment before the tomb of Innocent III, perhaps the most competent of the popes. As I wandered about back towards the Gregorian University where I have lived these years, I noted with pleasure that the lovely Tritone Fountain was finally working again after years of dryness due to repair. And I also walked by the fountain in front of the Viminale, which suddenly seemed to me to be of especial beauty. There is nothing quite like this City of Fountains.

And so I said good-bye also to various people at the Gregorian. The old tailor, a portly layman, who has pressed my pants and sewed rips and buttons for me, said to me in farewell, "*La vita è breve, Padre.*" Life is short—a fact and a philosophy not from the Gregorian's philosophers but from its normal working men.

And then I saw Father Charles Boyer (who has since died), a really great and productive old French priest, our spiritual father. He was then ninety-two or ninety-three. I said something silly like, "Well, I will see you again." He looked at me calmly and peacefully and replied, with much more Christian realism than mine, "*Ci vediamo in Paradiso*"—we shall see one another in Paradise. This too is what we ultimately believe in this City.

And finally at our porter's lodge, I said my good-bye to Brother Bradicich. He does so much quietly and effectively for all of the men at the Gregorian, things that the likes of myself never imagine have to be done, things without which the place simply falls apart. I thanked him for all the things he did for me over the years.

Brother answered with his shy smile and evident humility, "*Facciamo per tutti*"—we do the same thing for everyone. This too is another deep sentiment of our faith in its own way, a sense of the quality existing within the brotherhood. Another friend arrived for a visit. He told me that grace is more important than nature or justice. And that is about what the City of Rome has meant to me.

And so I walked by the Trevi Fountains for the last time. I did not throw in any coin—not, I think, because I am not sentimental but perhaps because I am. I have left this city each year for twelve years and never tossed in the traditional coin. I always came back before.

Rome is a place in which, when you leave it, you leave part of yourself. This is because when you arrived, part of you was already here. What you learned in the meantime was that from humanity there are many shadows, but from God much light. Ultimately, this is enough, even in this Eternal City.

5

On Old Age

Over on MacArthur Boulevard in Washington one day, I went into a local post office for a dollar's worth of stamps. The lady gave me five of a then-new issue of twenty-cent stamps on which were two elderly grandparents smiling tenderly at their two grandchildren. The reddish-brown stamp was called "Aging Together".

The following day along the bicycle path by the Potomac near the Kennedy Center, I almost ran into two of our sprightly seventy-year-old Fathers peddling rapidly into this lovely late Summer scene. Meanwhile, the Human Life Foundation had sent me a reprint of John Paul II's address on *Active Aging*, which he had given at Castel Gandolfo on September 5, 1980. So I sat down to read it, figuring, of course, that it would never apply to me.

The subject of old age is a perennial one, no doubt. For each of us, it is just a "matter of time", as they say. *The Republic* of Plato in fact began with a discussion about old age. "There is nothing which for my part I like better, Cephalus, than conversing with aged men; for I regard them as travellers who have gone a journey which I too may have to go . . ." Socrates remarked.

Cicero's wonderful essay "On Old Age" is something I try to have all my freshman classes read for a number of reasons, political and humanistic. This famous essay of Cicero, the Roman orator and philosopher, is one essay nineteen-year-olds like very much, perhaps not unsurprisingly, perhaps because they know that Socrates was right about our wanting to know something of the road along which we are already traveling at nineteen.

The Holy Father, I suppose, would put himself in the category of "an old man", so he can talk to the subject with experience. Old age, of course, is something that happens to each of us sooner or later, provided nothing stops our life cycle at any point from our conception on. And there is a point in saying that we are each equal in death, no matter at what period in our lives we die. God never said there was a different destiny for us depending on our age when we happen to die.

The Church encourages the elderly, the Pope said, "to look with realism and serenity on the role that God has assigned to them". And as the postage stamp implied, "The elderly are meant to be a part of the social scene, their very existence gives an insight into God's creation and the functioning of society. The life of the aging helps to clarify a scale of human values."

I remember as a boy worrying about how "old" my father, who died when he was sixty-one, was. He must have been all of thirty at the time I was worrying about his case! Yet, as we get older, life begins to bear certain reminders we do not notice the first time around. A couple of summers ago, I went to Magic Mountain in Southern California with my little grandnieces, Lisa and Caroline, along with their mother—with whom I could recall going to a park when she was about the same age.

A friend of mine in Washington was recently told by her ninety-year-old mother's doctor that, because of her mother's forgetfulness, it would be best to arrange for a nursing home. With much effort, my friend found a place, only to have her mother adamantly refuse to go. "She suddenly started to remember a lot more things", my friend laughed. We should not romanticize old age too much, I suppose. I remember my dear stepmother, when she was about eighty-four, remarking to me, after recounting how several of her friends were sick or dying, "They say these are supposed to be the 'golden years'. Well, they are not." Often, it is not clear what is best for aging people.

We live in a culture, lest we forget, which in many sectors has moved into position all the rationalization necessary to empower the state to declare the elderly worthless and therefore eliminate them quietly. We are not there yet, but the theory is about. Already we are frequently hearing of hospitals which put still-alive aborted fetuses or deformed infants aside in a room to starve to death.

We are already hearing of the same "mercy" for the old. The "legal" death of the elderly is only the other side of the "legal" death of the fetus. The elderly ought, in principle, to be the first to reject abortions, since they are surely slated to be next in this grizzly order of things.

Cicero, to return to more pleasant topics, felt that farming would be a good thing to do in old age. "A well-kept farm is the most useful thing to do in the world, and also the best to look upon. And age, far from impeding enjoyment of your farm, actually increases its pleasure and fascination. For nowhere else in the world can an old man better find sunshine or fireside for his warmth, shade and running water to keep himself cool and well."

There is something about an old man or woman in a garden making things grow, I think, that makes Cicero's words ring true. Perhaps it is the idea that they want to leave the world more beautiful; perhaps it is that somehow they sense that life and everlasting life are in harmony.

The old, John Paul II said, are "a part of God's plan for the world, with their mission to fulfill, their unique contributions to make, their problems to solve, their burdens to bear".

And Cicero likewise affirmed, "I am not sorry to have lived, since the course my life has taken has encouraged me to believe that I have lived for some purpose. But what nature gives us is a place to dwell in temporarily, not one to make our own. When I leave life, therefore, I feel as if I'm leaving a hostel rather than a home."

Scripture reminds us of the same thing, that we are merely wayfarers and pilgrims in this world. And the Pope adds that the elderly should appreciate "the mystery of human death, realistically to be accepted, but radically transformed in the Paschal Mystery of the Lord Jesus".

This sense of personal meaning, of individual death, of a hostel or inn, not a permanent home, of our passingness, is ultimately why we cannot be content either with this world or with those theories that suggest this world and its arrangements are all there is.

6

A Scottish Walk

The difference between a small town and a small city is as fundamental as the difference between a small city and a large metropolis. I grew up in a small town—Knoxville, in Iowa—on the basis of which some of my friends think they understand the famous saying that goes, "You can take the boy from the country, but you cannot take the country from the boy." Well, that is all right, I think.

Too, I have lived in some of the great cities of the world for extended periods—San Francisco, Ghent in Belgium. I was over a decade in Rome, and most recently in Washington. I love both small towns and large cities. In the former, I like the sense of rootedness; in the latter, I love their infinite variety and complexity. But there is another kind of a place, perhaps more charming and human than either a small town or a huge city, a place you might feel Aristotle or Plato was talking about, a place like Orvieto in Italy, or Lausanne in Switzerland, or Bamburg or Würzburg in Germany, or Salzburg in Austria, or Salisbury in England.

These middling places are monuments to mankind's genius; these are the small cities, places that bear within them much of the homeyness we associate with the small towns we came from—along with the variety and charm of the large city. Since I have been on the East Coast, for almost a decade now, I have found two small cities that I begin to think are sort of ideals of small cities. These are, first, Annapolis in Maryland, with its port, the State Capital, the spires of several churches, the Treaty of Paris Inn, St. John's College, the Naval Academy; and secondly, Alexandria in Virginia.

Both are beautiful cities visually, not merely picturesque like, say, New Hope in Pennsylvania, but in addition vital centers of activity, rather like the Monterey Peninsula in California, near where my brother and sister live (though Monterey has the disadvantage of being many cities or towns, so it lacks a unity that Alexandria or Annapolis has).

To be a city, there needs to be more than just quaintness, or history, or business, or education, or politics, or religion, or recreation, or military power. A city needs rather a subtle combination of all, the life that comes from the mixture of each of these elements in differing proportions, from the sense of the whole, including the whole world, and God too.

All of this I was thinking about because I chanced to go to the annual Christmas Scottish Walk in Alexandria, on a rainy, blustering, later clearing, day. Alexandria was founded by Scottish settlers in the eighteenth century, and it is a place that has a civic memory, one of the essential elements of a real city. Alexandria's "Sister City" is Dundee in Scotland, itself a reminder that so much more than America itself is needed to remember even America.

The Scottish Walk is, I suppose, what we would normally call a "parade" to open Christmas Season. Yet the very word "Walk" implies much more. We should "walk", "process" through our towns and cities at times "in style". We should take a look at them in their best. We should take the time to "see" the place in which we live and move.

We should, likewise, look at our kind "on occasion", at those who are before us precisely to be looked at. And most of all, on a Scottish Walk, we also wonderfully hear the sounds— the drums, the bagpipes. These are led by the Major, enhanced by the finery of Scottish color, the dignity of Scottish manhood.

Visually, Alexandria is a very beautiful small city, with street names like Princess and Duke and King and St. Asaph, with plaques on houses with names like Light Horse Harry Lee, a name I have always somehow loved for its very sound. To me, and I suppose to all Scotsmen, of which, alas, I am not one, there is no sound on this earth quite like the bagpipe, with the accompanying drums. The Alexandria Walk, fortunately, had plenty of pipers, along with some fifes and drums, with the colors of the Scottish Realm.

When they all marched into Alexandria's lovely Market Square for the Ceremonial Addresses and the massed Pipers, there was an almost unequaled majesty about it. A visiting friend was enchanted by it all, as was I. We went to the Presbyterian Meeting House for Noon Service; again "piped in" were the Bible, the Ministers, the Members of the St. Andrew's Society. The sermon was a fine one, given by a genuine Scotsman, a Campbell.

From there, still hearing pipes, we went to the Elks Club to listen to the Delaware Pipers; in the Fire House we bought a "Bridie", which was so very good on a cold day. The nearest thing to a Scottish pub that we could find was "Ireland's Own", already happily filled with disbanded Pipers "feeling no pain", as they say, even in Scotland.

Amidst the chatter, the noise, the eating, the smells, the crowd suddenly began to hear pipes coming closer and closer. There is just no sound like it—distant pipes coming ever closer. Then suddenly, into the pub marched the kilt-clad MacAlpine's Pipers, solemnly, yet to cheers and good cheers.

They played classic bagpipe music in a setting that makes you glad pubs were invented. Then, having played for us for a while, the Pipers, equally solemnly, marched out as we heard the music fade into nothingness.

I said to my friend, "It's how you come in and how you go out that matters."

"And what it is you do in the meantime, that you remember", was the response, "what it is you listen to."

The Scottish Walk in Alexandria, in a small city, in Virginia—in a place in this world, a place made lovely by the Potomac, by the people who live there, because others before them have lived there, Scotsmen too, mindful of how they come in and how they go out, how they walk solemnly on their streets, from Washington Street to Wolfe, on to St. Asaph, to Cameron, to Fairfax, and to Market Square; and the massed Pipers, with memories of mystical glory in the strains of "Bonnie Lassie" . . .

Indeed, it is how you come in and how you go out that counts. And yet, it is what you do in the meantime, in the loveliest of small cities, on this very earth, where we are wayfarers even at home.

7

The Southern Epitaph

Russell Hittinger is a friend whose father, grandfather, and other relatives are buried in Arlington Cemetery. Some time ago, he had mentioned to other friends of mine, Michael Jackson and Terry Hall, the existence, somewhere in Arlington National Cemetery in Washington, of a monument to Southern soldiers. I believe Michael or Terry even asked me to translate the Latin inscription on it. This is now very vague in my mind, but I do recall one of them telling me that the inscription was most curious and had to do with Cato and the gods in the cause of the South.

Largely because of a section in Josef Pieper's book *Scholasticism* on Boethius, the sixth-century Roman politician and philosopher, I assigned as a final book on Rome, for a Spring Semester course on "Classical Political Theory", Boethius' *De Consolatione Philosophiae*, one of the most widely read books in the history of the West. Boethius was sentenced to die by the Emperor Theodoric in 525 A.D. *On the Consolation of Philosophy* tried to explain this dire event to Boethius and to all of us who read him still.

Now, the book we read prior to Boethius was Tacitus' *Annals*, that most sobering, powerful account of the lives of the first four Roman emperors and their extraordinary women, as devastating an indictment of moral and political corruption as has ever been written. In recounting Nero's astonishing reign, Tacitus had spoken of the poet Lucan, who was fatefully annoyed because Nero himself pretended to be a legitimate poet. Nero finally resolved this little problem by doing away with Lucan. I did have a few pages of Lucan in an anthology somewhere, on Julius Caesar, but thought no more of the matter until I came across a reference to Lucan in Book Four of Boethius.

Condemned, Boethius was trying to marshal arguments to sustain and understand his plight. (On this point, read again the epigraph, taken from Johnson's *The Idler*.) Then "Philosophy" in the dialogue asked Boethius, "Has not our fellow philosopher Lucan told us how 'the conquering cause did please the gods, but the conquered, Cato'?" I read this passage over a couple of times trying to recall where I had heard it.

Suddenly, I felt sure it had to do with the Southern Monument in Arlington Cemetery, which, I thought, Michael Jackson had told me was just inside the Fort Meyer Gate. The footnote indicated that this famous passage was from Lucan's *Pharsalia* (I, 128). It referred to Julius Caesar's victory in 46 B.C. at Thapsus, when Cato, the representative of Roman virtue, saw the Republican cause was doomed. He committed suicide rather than endure Caesar.

So on a lovely April day, I told the morning class that immediately after class I was going to walk across Key Bridge, into the cemetery, to check on this Monument. I climbed into the cemetery by the Fort Meyer Gate and roamed around for about a half hour looking for it. Nobody seemed to be around. Finally, as I was about to go out the Memorial Gate, I spotted a cemetery service vehicle with two workers in it. I waved them down. Neither man had heard of the place. But I assured them it was there, on the authority of Jackson, Hittinger, and Hall. When another service truck came by, the two men honked it down. "Go talk to that guy; he's in charge of grave locations." "Just my man", thought I to myself.

I described what I wanted. He said there was some kind of a Southern Monument on the other side of the cemetery. "Hop in." He told me the Kennedy graves were still the most popular sites in the cemetery next to that of the Unknown

Soldier—a monument that always reminds me somehow of Lincoln's "Gettysburg Address" and its probable inspiration, Pericles' "Funeral Oration", from the Peloponnesian War. In both, speeches to the fallen unknown are forever enshrined. I introduced myself. He replied, "My name is Kennedy—no relation." I liked him.

We got to the Monument. It is in a well-kept, separate area. The Southern graves, usually with just the name, state, and CSA inscription, are in a circle around it. The Monument had been designed by Moses Ezekiel in Rome in 1912 and cast in Berlin. In retrospect, that almost seems eerie. Moses Ezekiel is buried next to it.

The Monument is quite large, noble; a womanly figure is on top. It was dedicated by the Confederate Daughters of America to their fathers and brothers. And there in Latin, no translation, was indeed the passage from Lucan through Boethius, which I showed to Mr. Kennedy. The spare Latin read "*Victrix causa diis placuit, sed victa, Catoni.*" It struck me that, in 1912, the educated Southerner probably could have translated that, and some even knew, unlike myself, where it was from.

What did it mean? This is what Hittinger, Hall, and Jackson had wondered about. The Southern ladies probably did not get the passage secondhand from Boethius, where it was used as an example to explain the difference between God's judgments and ours in human events. Lucan undoubtedly meant to praise Cato, the Stoic philosopher, who preferred death to tyranny.

What about the Southern ladies, Christians all, nearly? No doubt, the Southern ladies did not intend to suggest that the Southern men they loved committed suicide. What they meant was that, while the gods decreed the Union victory, still the defeated preferred Cato, preferred death to what was perceived as tyranny. Maybe that was why it was left in Latin; few would catch its nuances, except now and then some young philosophers.

I walked back to Georgetown through Fort Meyer. As I recrossed Key Bridge, I thought of Robert E. Lee, on whose land Arlington Cemetery now stands, crossing a bridge nearby on April 20, 1861, to tender his resignation from the Federal Army because he could not fight against his own people. I have a book of Lee's letters, which Father Cornelius Monacell gave me in San Francisco several years ago. I read it for a while after I returned home.

In July of 1863, Lee's own son was captured by the Union forces. Lee wrote to his mother, "We must bear this additional affliction with fortitude and resignation, and not repine the will of God. It will eventuate in some good that we know not of now. We must bear our labours and hardships manfully." I thought, "How like the spirit of the Romans, how even like Boethius' Philosopher, were these words." The Southern ladies chose well, even "manfully", as Lee told his own mother. In the end, "*Victrix causa diis placuit, sed victa, Catoni.*"

*

8

On the Practicality of One Green Sock

A couple of years ago, one of my sisters gave me a pair of fluffy, dark green socks for Christmas. Now, as my feet look terrific in green, I was quite pleased with them. However, these very socks occasioned a great crisis of self-confidence in my life. Like most other Americans, I suppose, I do not pride myself so much on being smart (questionable in any case) but on being practical. Nobody cares in the slightest if I can recite backwards, say, the Second Book of Aristotle's *Metaphysics*—which, incidentally, I can't, forward either.

But everyone is quite disconcerted if I cannot figure out where to put the coins into a BART (the subway in San Francisco) ticket machine or what button to push to get the darn ticket out after inserting the money. This is a simple operation, I understand, designed by the engineers of BART to accommodate the mentality of the average two-year-old. Thus, I will never forget the look on a lady's face at the Eighth and Market Street stop in San Francisco as she took my rejected dollar bill and turned it right side up so it would go into the machine as it is supposed to—one of those "Oh, you-poor-man" looks.

Anyhow, as in the similar case of pairs of blue, gray, and black socks, over the course of several months of washings, one of the green socks just disappeared. As our culture does not tolerate a green and a blue sock on the same pair of human feet, I invested in another hopefully matching pair. You cannot match them, however, let me clue you in, in case you are wondering. No two pairs of socks are exactly the same color.

But not too long after this incident, one of these new green socks was also missing. I was amazed and annoyed. Presently, after a sequence of lost socks that definitely proved the existence of original sin, if not Old Nick himself, I have four or five green socks, none of which is exactly the same shade, or style, or even size as any of the others.

After some time, naturally, I began to wonder where these missing green socks might have gone. Why was it I had accumulated so many non-matching socks? The robbery motive, on the whole, had to be excluded. I live in a religious community, a group generally not noted for thievery, each of whose inhabitants, as far as I know, has socks. Besides, who would want only one sock?

Further, some of these socks disappeared in the laundry room at Xavier Hall at the University of San Francisco, others in the laundry machines at Georgetown. As I do my own laundry, it means either the machines must be eating them up, or I must be negligent somehow.

Finally, after much searching for the missing items and explaining to my sceptical friends why the socks I wear do not always match—I am a little shaky on the things of this world anyhow—I decided there must be a scientific, non-moral explanation. That is, no one would want to steal them. I am the only one involved in routine processes of placing my socks in the washer and later transferring them to the dryer, thence back to my shelves until I need a clean pair of non-matching dark green socks.

At last, after some reflection, I believe my rusty, but, according to the philosophers, naturally deductive mind came up with a possible solution. Static electricity! You see, someone once told me that "what goes up, must come down". I never thought to question the principle at all. In college, I learned about the principle of causality, and in theology out in Los Gatos, California, I pondered Divine Providence. Both of these experiences led me astray.

I assumed for years, more than I care to count, that, if I looked at the bottom of a washer or dryer, all the things originally put inside it would end up on the bottom by virtue of the principle that heavier-than-air objects fall. I forgot about static electricity and wetness. And I was not prepared to question the law of gravity. One Galileo incident was enough.

Well, as you might suspect, the law of gravity let me down. I began to find, unaccountably, socks on the top of the dryer cylinder. Suddenly, the light dawned in the darkness of my mind. So that was what happened to my dark green socks! That must have meant, furthermore, that whoever used the washer or dryer after I did ended up with the extra green sock, assuming it eventually fell to the bottom.

And I can well imagine the puzzlement of a confrere over the fact that, whenever he did his laundry, an extra green sock appeared. He might have thought it was an omen, or a joke, or a miracle, even. I don't know. He may have begun to look askew at the Speed Queen Washer.

I now minutely search the machines for socks stuck on the top and thus do not anticipate losing any more. If I do, I will have to come up with a new theory. Justification is not by works, anyhow, as Luther said, not by works or socks.

However, there is something to be said for a little horse sense, something I never knew the nags had until I first went with my brother to Bay Meadows Race Track to note the skill with which they relieved him of his two-dollar bets.

Religion is usually pictured as a noble and lofty thing. Yet I sometimes think that the ultimate justification for Christianity has to do with a kind of practicality that finds missing socks, or at least finds why they are missing (I never actually found any of my missing ones).

Trivial things are trivial. The world does not rise or fall over one green sock. Nevertheless, its absence must be figured out somehow. A foot—namely, yours—is better for it. Little things are serious, yet to be taken lightly.

How to be able to make the world serious enough to do something about it, yet light enough to be free of it, is the central problem of all faith—of all lack of faith too, for that matter. The best argument for Christianity, I suspect, is precisely this: that there are serious things to do, yet nothing we do so binds that this seriousness is all there is.

One green sock means one other green sock is missing. If we did not have the first, we probably would not bother to look for the second. If we never missed anything, it would never occur to us to realize what we have. And, like my green socks, what we have is, in its depths, given to us.

9

Radiance

In Trenton, not too long ago, not far from the State of New Jersey government buildings, by the Delaware River, I was in a lovely old stone church, beautiful inside, the oldest Catholic church in that state, as its good pastor, Monsignor Leonard Toomey, told me. Sacred Heart, as I looked it up, dated from 1814, in a place where my friends, whom I was visiting, went to grammar school, albeit long, long, long after the church's founding! As I walked out of the sacristy, after concelebrating the eleven o'clock Sunday Mass with the monsignor, I noticed that he was about to baptize (still perhaps the most lovely of our sacraments) several infants.

I went over briefly to see more closely the first baby as the parents brought her up to the baptismal font for Monsignor Toomey to give her this gift she would spend the rest of her life wondering about. She was dressed in white, with a cute bonnet. Her mother told me, if I recall correctly, that her name was Emily, a name I quite like. She was maybe a month old, and I touched her head just to prove again, mainly to myself, that anything so dear could be real. She was an absolutely radiant child. She rather took my breath away—I was merely walking by on the way to the front door of the church, quite unprepared to glimpse such unexpected beauty, though I have come to realize beauty is always unsuspected. We realize, I think, that the vivid beauty and innocence of the human child do not come from us, even if we be its parents.

For some time now, I tend to look at a child such as this one—beautiful and whole as she was there suddenly before me in her mother's arms—and know she could have been quite legally destroyed only a few months before without a sound of law or pity, except perhaps for Dr. Nathanson's film, *Silent Scream*. Thank God for parents who defy such now-legal deeds, who carry what was theirs from conception now in their arms. Those who do not, and those who assist at the destruction of early human life, will be haunted forever, I suspect, by the radiant Emilys of this world who were not allowed to exist among us as was their right and glory, but who may now be with the God for whom each of us was created from the beginning.

Yet, here I was, in Sacred Heart Church, in Trenton, not thinking of any of this. I had just had a good conversation with a parishioner in the sacristy about the economics of vending machines, the gentleman's business. I had learned a lot, in fact, about the problems of the small vendor. And suddenly, on the way out, I was sort of awestruck by a chance seeing of this lovely child, whom I will never see again. I really did not see her parents or grandparents, just her, from the nowhere of our origins.

Josef Pieper, in his extraordinary book, *The Silence of Saint Thomas*, has a long discussion about the nature of creature-hood, in which we all, including this little Emily, exist. "It is quite impossible for us, as spectators, so to speak," Pieper wrote,

> to contemplate the emergence of things from "the eye of God." Since this is so, our quest for knowledge when it is directed toward the essence of things, even of the lowest and "simplest" order, must move along a pathway to which there is, in principle, no end. The reason for this is that things are *creaturae*, that the inner lucidity of being has its ultimate and exemplary source in the boundless *radiance* of Divine knowledge.[1]

[1] Josef Pieper, *The Silence of Saint Thomas* (Chicago: Regnery, 1957), 63.

I read this passage from Pieper on the Amtrak *Palmetto*, leaving Trenton at 9:21 A.M. for Washington. I thought to myself, well, of course, this is what I saw in little Emily, newly born and baptized, a beauty in a tiny creature whose full origin reaches, directly, to infinity itself. This is why it was given to us and why we dare not touch it, except to touch her to make us realize that such things exist. We are blessed with them because we are struck by them, by their lucidity, their inner light, which is already there.

In T. S. Eliot's "Ash Wednesday"—which I try, ritually, to read on that Beginning Lenten Day every year—it says:

> Because of the goodness of the Lady
> and because of her loveliness, and because
> she honours the Virgin in meditation,
> we shine with brightness . . .

Ever since Aristotle, philosophers have tried to account for the something "more" that exists in all things beyond what we ourselves might think they "need". The attempt, we realize in seeing such a one as this little Emily, is one that must be made.

We live in a world crowded with people who maintain that we have been "given" too little. Poor, desperate souls! This is *not* our problem. We live in a world in which we can hardly imagine how much we have been given—and even when we succeed a little to suspect this from the reaches of space to the radiance of Emily, we are tempted to create our own parsimonious world instead. And if we do insist on so doing, so making our own world, well, we are left with merely our own choices, our own creation. If we destroy millions of our little Emilys before they see our daylight, we are left with the nothingness of their absence, without the radiance of the little one I actually saw and touched by chance in an old church in Trenton, thinking I already knew all about my world.

IO

The Park

One wet Sunday afternoon, I was headed out the back door of
Xavier Hall at the University of San Francisco, going nowhere
in particular, as is my wont. By chance, I spotted Father Lloyd
Burns just pulling onto Parker Street. So I hitched a ride—to
"wherever you're going", as I told him.

Well, he was going to a wake in Stonestown, but as I was
just not ready to walk back from a wake, I got off at Ninth and
Lincoln, to wander into the lovely Strybing Arboretum in
Golden Gate Park, a favorite place of mine.[1] It was mostly
empty. Rather cold, a slight drizzle.

As this was the first time since 1963 that I had been in California after the middle of January (it was 1984), I had been
looking forward to Winter and Spring in San Francisco again.
Somehow, I thought I had been all through this part of the
park, but I turned off a path leading by the Cactus Garden and
into the very green "communities" of pine and grass. I think
the green of the grass in the middle of the California Winter,
when there has been lots of rain, is just spectacular, especially
on a cloudy day.

This section of the park was fenced in and well-cared-for.
Everything seemed to be named, even in the most obscure
areas. I like that, even though botanical names do not do much

[1] See James V. Schall, "On Building Cathedrals and Tearing Them Down", in
The Praise of 'Sons of Bitches': On the Worship of God by Fallen Men (Slough, England: St. Paul Publications, 1978), 34.

for me. I think calling, as I saw a sign there do, a Douglas fir a "Pseudotsugas something or other" is not enlightening to my darkness.

This sort of ignorance of mine reminds me of a series in an old *Peanuts* I chanced to buy (for twenty-five cents at the time) at McDonald's Used Book Store on Turk Street, a perfectly wondrous, chaotic book emporium for finding things you never knew existed—which is sort of what parks are for too, not to mention the world itself.

Anyhow, Linus, in this *Peanuts*, was stooped over in some grass and gravel. Lucy said, "Here's a nice pebble, Linus. Take it home and observe it." Linus, perplexed, was next seen looking at the pebble, as Lucy explained, "The fascinating thing about pebbles is their growth, for some grow up to be stones, while others grow up to be rocks."

Lucy then walked away from a rather astonished Linus, saying to him, "You shall hope, of course, that it grows up to be a rock, for a pebble that grows up to be a stone is like a youth who has gone astray." Finally, Linus is seen alone in the gravel and grass, looking for his pebble. "Sigh," he uttered, "I have so much to learn."

Well, that is just about how I felt in Golden Gate Park that day, surveying the names of every plant that grows on this green earth and hardly able to tell a "ficus" from a "malus", of which there are lots in Golden Gate Park.

I am a big fan of gardens and parks, Golden Gate Park in particular. Parks and gardens are our way of saying how we think nature ought to look. There are, no doubt, scads of folks who think nature looks fine, like Marin County backwaters or Nebraska plains, where there are few people.

"We should have left the space between Fulton and Lincoln in sand dunes, as it was two hundred years ago", some enthusiast would say. But most people come to this place to see the park, not the sand dunes—not that I have anything against sand dunes, like those by Pescadero Beach, down Coast Highway One from Golden Gate Park.

In San Francisco I am often on the No. 5 Bus coming up

from Market Street to the University. On this line there are obviously many tourists from, say, Ladue, Missouri, or Keokuk, Iowa, maps in hand, confused in face, wondering if it is possible to pass right by the park without seeing it.

Finally, one tourist bravely walks up to the driver and asks, loudly, for the jillionth time, "Is the park on this route?" As the poor tourist from Keokuk goes back to his seat, still not sure, about ten people begin to tell him and his wife what to see there. It is sort of nice, this common good.

Parks ought to be two things—beautiful and safe. You can have your own garden, but you cannot have your own park. A park somehow needs to be a place where everyone can go, but only on terms of quiet civilization. A park is a park, a place where certain things are particularly set aside when you go into it. And a park needs to be big enough to have quiet places and corners to get lost in.

Parks, I think, remind us of Eden—places where man and *natura* are at harmony, or at as much so as is possible for us mortals. Yet weeds grow there too, even if the flowers of one continent are the weeds of another. Parks need constantly to battle the elements and man just to keep themselves what they are designed to be. Without meticulous, constant care, a garden or a park is soon a weed-patch or a desert or a jungle, or even a sand dune. Probably, there is nothing more forlorn than an unkept park, a symbol, in its way, of The Fall.

Back in 1955, C. S. Lewis wrote to a "child in America": "We had our first frost last night—this morning the lawns are all grey, with a pale bright sunlight on them, wonderfully beautiful. And somehow *exciting*. The first beginning of Winter always excites me; it makes me want adventure." No doubt, if we read the papers, we do not know what Winter is in a San Francisco, compared to Lewis' England or, say, Minot, in North Dakota, where my cousin lives.

Yet I think our parks somehow enable us to participate in this excitement and adventure of change in season, something of the eternal adventure of all creation in harmony, the local adventure of a tourist finding at last the beautiful Golden Gate

Park, or the excitement of an old hand like myself finding a glen of green Winter grass, not expected to exist. Yet it does, and we have found it, seen it, walked on it.

The Roots of Joy

One of Ogden Nash's delightful poems is entitled: "I Can't Have a Martini, Dear, But You Take One, or Are You Going to Sit There Guzzling All Night?" On reading such a wonderfully convoluted title, we just laugh, then wonder why we do, or even how it is possible that beings can laugh.

Just why things are funny—they are, after all—brings up questions of the profoundest moment. We live in a world that seems to be getting more somber. Yet we live in a universe in which laughter is possible. We know this because we have heard our dearest friends laugh.

However, it makes a good deal of difference what kind of a cosmos we think we live in, even when we laugh. If we be really logical, after all, some deterministic views of the world do not allow us to laugh, if we are serious about their implications. A necessary "laughter" is not, after all, laughter at all.

People may remember, or have heard on a replay on Old-Time Radio, Molly McGee's famous quip, "'Tain't funny, McGee." And this is enough to remind us that even not being funny when we think we are hilarious is itself quite humorous—if you follow me.

We have heard a lot of talk about the world's being blown up, some of it quite amusing. We are told, nevertheless, that it isn't funny. Yet, if we think about it, if the world of our human condition is not somehow the context of humor, even if the darn thing is blown up, then we have a very strange philosophy. We have, in other words, a problem with our thought, not with our given world.

Christianity thinks the world will end sooner or later. It seems even to expect this ending to be rather spectacular and full of fire. I saw an interesting essay in the *Policy Review*[1] called "Apocalypse Now: What Fundamentalists Believe about the End of the World". Likewise, each of us ends his life in turn. We are but passing beings. Yet, we are gripped by this curious fit of laughter, almost as if we want to laugh about it and cannot.

A student of mine wrote to me not too long ago:

> Have you ever had the unfortunate experience of wanting to laugh very hard when you were somewhere you couldn't? It used to happen to me all the time when I was a little girl at Mass.
>
> Just the other day, my poetry teacher was pointing out the more serious mistakes we had made on our papers. He pointed out that one of us had misspelled the poet's name throughout the paper. It was me, of course.
>
> I had misread his handwriting, and written a three-page paper about, not Clough's, but "Plough's Decalogue". I really wanted to laugh, because it seemed the most unexpected mistake.
>
> And although I never would have recognized the mistake, I am sure that for the professor, it was like reading a paper about John K. Fennedy! Unfortunately, no one said anything funny . . .

Laughing when we cannot, ought not—we wonder if this is not somehow our very condition.

Even if we depart from this world one at a time, nevertheless what matters still is how we look at our destiny. There really is no joy in the idea that the earth just continues on as it is *ad infinitum* with no real transformation, no real ending. If this world is indeed the end, then our laughter is hollow anyhow, almost like that horrid laughter we sometimes associate with wickedness and hopelessness.

[1] Fall 1986.

Easter is the Christian Feast that grounds our joy and our laughter. Ultimately, this is what distinguishes us from all else in Creation. We are told that it is what we do on earth that counts, that our wills and our actions proceeding from them are ultimately what distinguishes each of us.

However true this may be in one sense, we can have lasting joy only if "what we do" is not our own final condition. Something must first be done to us. That there is something to hope for depends only secondarily on our doing or not doing. That there is everlasting life does not depend on us. All utopianism based on the claim that it does leaves us only with ourselves.

Chesterton said, "We awake at our birth staring at a very funny place. After serious examination of it, we receive two fairly definite impressions: the first, delight and the second, fear." This is, of course, the sudden realization that things are improbably funny because they stand against a background of chosen freedom, a freedom we can use in two ways, because we are beings of ultimate risk, that is, of ultimate drama.

Our delight has the same root as fear, that is, in the good itself. The world is a delightful and happy place because we can reject it. This means ironically that we know the good really can be ours, but only if we choose it. If the good existed but could not somehow be ours, we would only despair.

In an old *Peanuts*, Lucy overheard Charlie Brown, elbows on the table, head in hands, muttering wistfully, "Y'know, I'll bet if I were to disappear tomorrow, nobody would miss me." Lucy responded, earnestly, "Oh, I don't think that is true, Charlie Brown", who answered somewhat reassured, "You don't?" "No," Lucy continued, "I don't think that's strictly true at all." And in the final scene, she asserted to an obviously crushed Charlie Brown, "Even if you were to disappear *today*, nobody would miss you."

Easter is dedicated to the proposition that none of us, Lucy or Charlie Brown, ever disappears either today or tomorrow, even when we do disappear from this world itself tinged both with humor and sadness. Crucifixion and Resurrection in the

Christian tradition are parts of the same whole, which is why even our most sublime joys are touched by sorrows. And our sorrows are not ultimate, unless we make them so. The world is full of delight and fear, staring at this funny place in which we cannot always laugh.

Another of Ogden Nash's poems, "Piano Tuner, Untune that Tune", begins with this prophetic, funny line: "I regret that before people can be reformed, they have to be sinners." The astonishment is that this indeed is our condition. We do regret that we be sinners in need of reform—it is in such a world that the joy called Easter, Resurrection, the central doctrines of faith, exists.

If we think of the meaning of the Christian teaching about Easter, then we can, perhaps, put it in this logical fashion, to conclude:

1. I can't have a martini, Dear, but you take one.

2. We wake up at our birth staring at a very funny world.

3. Even if you were to disappear today, nobody would miss you.

4. I regret that before people can be reformed, they have to be sinners.

This is the Day the Lord has made, Rejoice!

12

On Keeping the Old Religion

James Boswell was in Wittenberg, in Saxony, on September 30, 1764, on his "Grand Tour" in Germany and Switzerland. He visited there the tombs of Luther and Melanchthon. The convent that housed the remains of these famous Protestant divines had, unfortunately, been "miserably shattered by the bombardments", but the tombs were still intact. Boswell liked Melanchthon, but Luther not much. Boswell occupied himself there by borrowing pen and ink from the woman who showed him the chapel.

Somewhat to the astonishment of the locals (which Boswell was not above deliberately provoking, moreover) he proceeded to stretch himself out prone on the Tomb of Melanchthon, where he calmly wrote a letter to Samuel Johnson, who did not like Luther either. Boswell suspected the selection of this outlandish writing desk rather than Luther's would please Johnson. Boswell, in fact, thought that Melanchthon was "the worthiest of all the reformers, with no private resentment to gratify". Boswell recalled of Melanchthon, "So mild was he that when his aged mother consulted him with anxiety on the perplexing disputes of the times, he advised her to keep the old religion."

To "keep the old religion", of course, is no mean feat, as I am sure even Melanchthon's mother found out. Part of the reason keeping the faith is difficult, I suppose, is because we do not pray about what we believe, about the substance of the doctrines themselves. On Laetare Sunday, March 19, 1939, in Paris, Raïssa Maritain had been to Mass celebrated by Père Bruno. In her *Journals*, she reflected:

> During Mass, I understood certain things about predestination. And that, at one moment or another of our life, we have to make a choice for the world or for Christ insofar as the latter is head of the world of grace, as opposed to *this world* of which Lucifer is the prince.[1]

She understood, in other words, that the knowledge of God does not free us from the choice of God in the context of our lives. In asking us to love him, God does not, in other words, ask us to cease taking the risk of being free, of being human.

In addition to praying about "keeping the old religion", we also must recognize that there are many conflicting ideas and faiths and temptations, including the case of predestination, striving for our attention. In Woody Allen's book, *Side Effects*, there is a posthumous account of one Sandor Needleman's life. Needleman, in Allen's recollection, was a sort of modern philosopher. "Human freedom for Needleman consisted of being aware of the absurdity of life. 'God is silent,' he was fond of saying 'now if we can only get man to shut up'." The doctrines of faith are our primary reasons for holding that we are free and that life is not absurd; and no doubt, man will not shut up on the subject. We can sympathize with Melanchthon's mother's perplexities even yet.

In the Third Part of the *Summa Theologiae*, Saint Thomas asked "Whether Christ, after the Resurrection, Had a True Body". Too few of us, I suppose, also pray over this very truth of our faith, and the opinions of the philosophers are noteworthy for only one thing on this topic: none of them is as shockingly wondrous as the faith itself. Thomas had no doubt about the topic and gave his reasons. He simply concluded, "If (Christ's) body was some sort of phantasm, there was not really

---

[1]*Journal of Raïssa Maritain*, ed. Jacques Maritain (Albany: Magi Books, 1975), 271.

a Resurrection, but only an apparent one." And if this latter is so, why bother? Saint Paul had said about the same thing.

At sometime in our lives we have to choose for or against the world of grace of which Christ is the head. Christianity does not hold, ultimately, that our external circumstances will obviate this decision. Whether we be in the Gulags in which a Solzhenitsyn ironically holds that faith turns out to be stronger than in free societies, or at a Mass with Père Bruno with Raïssa Maritain, or prone on the Tomb of Melanchthon writing to Samuel Johnson, we need to realize what it is our faith teaches us about the ultimate choice we have to make. Saint Thomas taught us that the Resurrection involves precisely us, not an apparent us. This is why God took the risk of putting us here in the first place, in this world of grace, which we can accept or reject.

God is silent, now if we can only get man to shut up. At one moment or another of our lives we have to make a choice for the world or for Christ insofar as the latter is the head of the world of grace. *Si autem eius [Christi] corpus fuisset phantasticum, non fuisset vera resurrectio, sed apparens.* If, with Melanchthon's good mother, we want to keep the old religion, we must pray about, think about this truth that the Resurrection of Christ was not just a phantasm or phantasy but a reality, one that makes our choice for or against Christ central in our lives. In the end, I think, not even Sandor Needleman would be content with a *corpus phantasticum*, however absurd it might sound to the philosophers or to the men who will not shut up.

13

Extraordinary Enough to Be Exciting

In his *Autobiography*, G. K. Chesterton, who, as he told us, was in despair as a young man, decided, finally, that he had enough of this pessimistic thought and decided to revolt against it. He found very little help from the standard sources.

> But as I was still thinking the thing out by myself, with little help from philosophy and no real help from religion, [he recalled], I invented a rudimentary and makeshift mystical theory of my own. It was substantially this: that *even mere existence, reduced to its most primary limits, was extraordinary enough to be exciting.* Anything was magnificent as compared with nothing.

These are remarkable lines. We have not arrived at thought, I think, until we have wondered whether what exists, including ourselves, might not exist. Or, as Eric Voegelin put it in his *Conversations*, there are two fundamental questions that precede all others: Why is there something rather than nothing? And why is this thing as it is and why is it not that thing?

Years ago, when I happened to be in a summer school in France, trying to square the circle, that is, pronounce French the way the Frenchmen do, I ran into a young German student whom I rather liked. But he had a problem. He was quite annoyed over the fact that no one ever consulted him about the question of his own existence and birth; that is, he seemed to have wanted to decide, ahead of time, whether he ought to exist or not.

Now, this position is utterly contradictory as a proposition, but it is quite revealing as an attitude to reality. Thus, in this view, if we are not first consulted about whether we want to exist, we are then justified in not blaming ourselves if we turn out badly.

The truth is, however, we are first given existence, our own and that of everything else. Then we are asked, more or less, what we are going to do about it and ourselves within everything else. What we "do" about it, furthermore, reveals what we decide to do with ourselves, what we decide to make ourselves to be. We do not decide "who" we are, for we are given this, our status in reality as human beings, not toads or some sort of fir tree. Others see us in this light as beings who act. They will praise or blame us on the basis of what we do with the reality, including our own, given to us through no instrumentality of our own.

Certain advantages accrue to us from the fact that, since we did not "make" or create ourselves, we can assume that others are in the same position. That is, the world is full of people who somehow find themselves given existence for no reason whatsoever, apparently, other than the fact that there they are. This means, I think, that if there is a plot to the world, we may be in it, but we did not construct it. We do not know how things will turn out on the last page, though we are inevitably in the story somehow.

In a very good book, really an extended conversation with John Paul II, the French journalist André Frossard remarked to the Holy Father, "even the most convinced Christians seem today to take from the Gospel only what can contribute to social change or to the expression of their individual freedom."[1] In his comments, John Paul II referred to a famous incident, during his visit to Paris, of a young man who asked at a rally of 90,000 young students about the Pope's own faith: "The young man in the Parc des Princes asked me: 'Holy Father, in whom do you believe? Why do you believe? What

[1] André Frossard, *"Be Not Afraid"* (New York: St. Martin's Press, 1984).

is it that is worth the gift of our life and what manner of being is this God that you adore?' "

I sometimes think that this Holy Father (John Paul II), who has probably talked to more young students than any other man in the history of mankind, is today the only public figure whom young people might have the courage to ask such questions with the expectation of getting an answer that conforms to reality.

Most people, I think, at one time or another read *The Lord of the Rings*. In some notes he made on Auden's review of this book, J. R. R. Tolkien wrote, "In *The Lord of the Rings* the conflict is not basically about 'freedom', though that is naturally involved. It is about God, and his sole right to divine honor." [2]

I have often wondered if there is any relationship between this remark of Tolkien's and that of Chesterton's about the excitement of existence as such. That is, what constitutes the source of this ever varied existence we experience but which we did not make ourselves? This is really the question the young man in Paris asked John Paul II. The real question is not about freedom or social change, but about the manner of being of God and of our relation to this. Tolkien understood this directly, and this constitutes the wonder of his tales.

In Jane Austen's *Mansfield Park*, there is a scene in which Fanny is taken into the chapel of the Rushworth Mansion, a disappointingly plain chapel, "a mere, spacious, oblong room fitted up for devotion". Fanny reacted with some disappointment: "This is not my idea of a chapel. There is nothing awful here, nothing melancholy, nothing grand. Here are no aisles, no arches, no inscriptions, no banners. No banners, cousin, to be 'blown by the night winds of Heaven'. No sign that 'a Scottish monarch sleeps below'."

Chesterton said that anything was magnificent compared to nothing. This sanity of the race reacts to this magnificence, in ourselves, in our origins, as though we were aware that here

[2] *The Letters of J. R. R. Tolkien* (Boston: Houghton Mifflin, 1981), 243.

something awe-ful, something grand is present. But we can react this way only if we understand that, though we do not have to be, we are. But if there is something that simply *is*, then, as Tolkien wrote in his tales, there is a source wherein we place our honor, in the manner of the being of God.

14

Sane and Glad

The lesson from Isaiah at Midnight Mass on Christmas reads: "Thou has increased their joy and given them great gladness." I am often struck by the fact that, in Christianity, joy and gladness are not so much a product of our own activities but something much more, something that happens when all that the Greeks might have meant by "happiness" is already fully present. Joy, even the fullest, can be "increased", and "great gladness" is not earned but given. However noble and worthy it is to "earn" something, and it is, however much we want our happiness to be precisely "ours", not someone else's, still the promise of Isaiah does not portend something we might have expected.

When Christianity applied these wondrous lines to the Incarnation of the Son of God, or rather, when Christianity came to understand that this joy and gladness are what was meant by the events in Bethlehem, we realized that here we had something we could not have had the slightest advance notice about. Nevertheless, here we have something that addresses what it is we really want if we could want it. Again, we realize that the roots of unbelief in Christianity are really not that it does not promise us enough, but rather that it promises us too much. We are, in truth, in our unbelief, sad, doubtful beings who turn away because we are given more than we desired.

In the passage from Saint John's Prologue, read at the Midday Mass on Christmas, it says that we shall receive "grace upon grace", almost as if to hint that we have no real idea about what is really best for us. And it is just as well that we don't, for otherwise we should undoubtedly choose something so much less than we are in fact given. We would think, in theory, that because we choose something, it is really, and for that very reason, better than something given to us, even if we too, eventually, have to choose what is given to us, grace upon grace. But it is not so. What is best is what is given to us, unexpectedly.

In my more playful moments, I have often thought that, among the intellectual journals, *Mad Magazine* came closer to right theoretical order, to *what is*, than, say, *Reason*, or *Mind*, or *Thought*. *Mad* begins with the derangement of reason and laughs at it, in the name of reason—wild reason, in *Mad*'s case. Chesterton was not too far away from the same sort of paradox when he pointed out that the mind that starts out to be completely and systematically natural, usually ends up, by itself, to be most unnatural. This result, Chesterton thought, was not a theoretical proposition, but an observation of what intellectuals came to hold.

Actually, all of this sort of musing was occasioned by some lines in Saint Augustine's *City of God* (XI, 22), which I came across the other day while preparing for class. The passage reads: "If proof is needed how much human nature loves to know and hates to be mistaken, recall that there is not a man who would not rather be sad but sane than glad but mad." I am sure Alfred E. Neuman and his friends at *Mad* would find Augustine a totally compatible character in this sentiment.

To be sure, it should be added that I read this passage out loud in class, to ask my ever amusing and good student which she would prefer, to be "sad but sane" or "glad but mad". Naturally, to the delight of the class, she chose "mad but glad". So we all laughed and proved Augustine's paradox, for you cannot laugh at my student's good wit without seeing the truth of Augustine's remark about what we really prefer.

Of course, there is a certain sadness to life, as Augustine often recounted. Yet it is, ultimately, gladness that we are about. In his autobiography, Josef Pieper recounted his first meeting as a young man with Romano Guardini. In 1920 or so, Pieper had gone to a kind of youth encampment in Berg Rothenfels. He wrote:

> And then, primarily through getting to know Romano Guardini, we encountered a hitherto unsuspected dimension of spiritual reality and proceeded to seize hold of it with passionate intensity. We came to understand what a "sacred sign" is in reality, and that, beyond all the stifling crassness of moralistic and doctrinaire talk, something real takes place in the sacramental/cultic celebration of the mysteries, something that, otherwise, can only be spoken about.[1]

At Christmas, what actually takes place in the Masses, the sacramental celebration, is real. The "reality" of this cultic event is itself the result of the Incarnation of the Son of God as a Child in Bethlehem.

This most unlikely Christmas event, then, and what it portends for us—for what it contains is what we hope for, what it is we are given: the increase of joy, the grace upon grace—is that our philosophies are sad because they are not sane enough. Our gladness is, to the world, a kind of madness, because the world cannot conceive of something that has been given through no invention or contribution of our own. "Madness" if you will, joy, saneness, as I prefer to call it, is the freedom and understanding to see that this joy is indeed what we are for, in the highest things, in the depths of the Christmas mystery.

[1] Josef Pieper, *No One Could Have Known: An Autobiography: The Early Years* (San Francisco: Ignatius Press, 1987), 39.

15

Mary Concannon

In June of 1978, I spent a lovely Friday with my three then-young nieces in Aptos in California. We went for a ride on the big Dipper roller coaster and the Loggers' Revenge on the Boardwalk in Santa Cruz. As my brother and sister-in-law were down at Santa Barbara for their eldest son's graduation from UCSB, the ladies were in charge of what we would do. So we tried to eat some Chinese food with chopsticks (they resorted to forks), and later they tried, unsuccessfully, to teach their improbable clerical uncle how to dance à la the then-popular Saturday Night Fever.

When I returned that evening to Xavier Hall at the University of San Francisco where I was staying, I found a letter from my old friends Bernard and Josie Concannon, from Solihull, in the West Midlands of England, just below Birmingham. The letter contained the sad news of their daughter Mary's death on the Feast of the Holy Innocents, December 28, 1977.

They had, indeed, written previously but heard that the post in "North America" wasn't altogether reliable, so they kindly wrote again, as they knew I would want to know. I never received the earlier letter, so I appreciated their second writing.

I met Mary Concannon when she was three. I had been doing my year of "tertianship"—a then-inexplicable part of Jesuit training—in Drongen, Belgium. For Lent of 1965, I was assigned to help out at St. Peter's Parish on High Street in Bloxwich near Walsall in Staffordshire, in England's so-called

"Black Country". I love English place names like that. Connected with the parish in this town was what the English call an "infants' school"—a grammar school to us.

English children used to fascinate me no end, and I could sit by the hour just chatting and listening to them speak that remarkable language, English, in a way I had never before imagined it could be spoken. The children thought I was a "Yankee" and were never quite sure what I was talking about—a difficulty, to be sure, my brothers and subsequent years of students at USF and Georgetown have also wondered about.

In the next parish was a regional Catholic "Secondary Modern School"—to us, a high school. At that time, Bernard Concannon was the assistant principal at Francis Martyn, this very secondary modern school. Over the years we became good friends.

Later on, when I passed through England every so often to or from Rome, where I was teaching at the Gregorian University, I would stay with Bernard and Josie and their five children. Their home was a place in which I always liked to be.

Mary Concannon was the second youngest child of Bernard and Josie. She had dark red hair, rather a frail child compared to her three sisters. Mary was very abrupt, even skittish. She was a challenging, unusual child somehow. I was always fascinated by her.

She even had a look of "pain" in her eyes, a sort of poignancy about her, or so it seemed to me, though I may now be reading this back into my earliest impressions of her, but I do not think so. From the very beginning, everyone talked about Mary in a special way.

About five years or so before I heard of her death, Bernard and Josie wrote saying that a large tumor had been discovered in Mary's brain, one evidently there all along. The operation was performed by the best surgeons in Britain, but the damage in general was severe. Yet Mary mostly recovered, or so it seemed.

She could go to special schools, live at home, grow up some. Mary's life was always tenuous after that. No one told me that in so many words, but I could tell it by her mother's manner, by the way Josie's many sisters would talk to Mary. I used to drop a card to Mary once in a while from Rome or San Francisco. Eventually, she would drop a card or letter back.

I remembered visiting Solihull once during this period. Bernard, Mary, and I took a delightful walk along the old canal paths dating back to the Industrial Revolution. I have a wonderful photo of Mary and her father. And I recall long hours of playing cards with Mary and her sisters. Mary used to teach me new card games, then proceed delightedly to beat me at them.

When I saw Mary after her operation, somehow all the pain in her eyes was gone, to be replaced by the most gentle, compassionate gaze. That sounds funny, but it is true. I remember how Mary made me think of the mystery of the suffering of the innocent; her death on the Feast of the Holy Innocents seemed symbolic of this.

Now, if Christianity means anything, it means that the suffering of the innocent should turn us toward God, not away from him. And this was so with Mary. On her memorial card there is a smiling photo of her taken in English schoolgirl uniform shortly before Christmas vacation of her last year, just before she died.

Mary used to play the violin—once I remember her Uncle Joe ruining her violin in a clown act at a happy family party. Mary just laughed, because she knew her uncle would get her an even better violin the next day, which, of course, he did. Her school made a display of the pottery she made, and she had top honors in art just before she died.

On Mary's memorial card there were also two hymns that Mary had copied out in her own hymnbook. I want to cite them here, as they solve so many mysteries and open so many others about Mary's life. This is the first poem:

> God's spirit is in my heart.
> He has called me and set me apart.
> This is what I have to do,
> What I have to do.

Go tell everyone the news
That the Kingdom of God has come.
And go tell everyone the news
That the Kingdom has come.

And this is the second poem:

O Jesus, thou hast promised
To all who follow thee,
That where thou art in glory
There shall thy servant be;
And, Jesus, I have promised
To serve thee to the end.
O give me grace to follow
My Master and my Friend.

The death of the young is tragic. Yet much is completed in a short time, as Scripture teaches us and Mary's life exemplified.

What I remember most about Mary was the way her eyes changed, and the voices of the people who talked to her. She was set apart, I think. I could easily hate a world in which what happened to Mary happened. I could—except for the fact that Mary herself did not. I suspect only when we understand her gentleness can we really begin to live as Mary now does.

16

On Conversation and Companionship

"For an encounter with another person, through acts of knowing and love, in freedom", the Polish Dominican philosopher Mieczyslaw Krapiec wrote in his remarkable book, *Philosophical Anthropology*, "presupposes precisely a personal 'I' who actualizes himself through interpersonal communications in the order of being." [1] This is, no doubt, a complicated way of saying that we are beings who seek a truth we did not make. We want to tell others about it simply because it is and is worth saying. This illuminates our 'I', who we are.

For this, we need leisure and the institutions of leisure—our homes, perhaps most of all, our walks, our places where nothing "useful" takes place, since our highest acts remain "beyond use". John Cage put it in Silence: "The highest purpose is to have no purpose." [2] The highest things exist in themselves. We do not want to go to any other place when we are already there where we want to go.

We need a civilization, in other words, in which we can speak freely and honestly to our friends who *listen*, not forgetting what Aristotle said about the difficulties of friendship.[3] Nothing, indeed, is more "uncivilizing" than the popular demand for instant friendship, though, as Plato said, it some-

[1] Mieczyslaw Krapiec, *Philosophical Anthropology* (New Britain, CT: Mariel, 1983), 244.

[2] John Cage, *Silence* (Cambridge, MA: MIT Press, 1986), 155.

[3] Aristotle, *Ethics*, books 8 and 9.

times can happen most suddenly.[4] Civilization is nothing less, as someone once said, than two or three friends chatting in a room.[5] Societies that lack this possibility, to recall Aristotle again, are already in the hands of a tyrant, one or many.

The great revelation of Christianity, as Eric Voegelin, among others (like Saint Thomas), has noted, cannot be understood without first grasping the import of Aristotle's position that we cannot be friends with God.[6] Aristotle had understood that the highest things exist in friendship, not in justice. He also knew that the "activity" of the First Mover consists in thinking and loving. He was not exactly "wrong" on either of these points, but reason had much difficulty in figuring out how he could be both right and wrong. Revelation indicated that there is "otherness" in God, an otherness of persons and that this God of persons has invited us, made it possible for us, to be his friends, a position made visible by the Incarnation itself. The Word was made flesh and dwelt amongst us.

But we will never understand the "answers" of revelation if we do not somehow have the experience of the questions. God insists on treating us as we are. We are given, in other words, a real life in which there is real love, knowledge, and passion; sometimes too, hatred, ignorance, and distaste. After some argument, Protagoras, in Plato's *Protagoras*, had refused to answer Socrates any more. For this refusal, Alcibiades chided Protagoras. This embarrassed Protagoras enough to allow Socrates to ask him:

> Do not imagine, Protagoras, that I have any other interest in asking questions of you but that of clearing up my own problems as they arise. For all men who have a companion are readier in deed, word, and thought, but if a man sees a thing when he is alone, he goes straightway seeking until he finds someone

[4] See Josef Pieper's wonderful book *Enthusiasm and the Divine Madness*, trans. Richard and Clara Winston (New York: Harcourt, 1964), chaps. VI and VII especially.

[5] Schall, *Redeeming the Time* (New York: Sheed and Ward, 1968), 216–27.

[6] Eric Voegelin, *The New Science of Politics* (Chicago: University of Chicago Press, 1952), 66.

to whom he may show his discoveries and who may confirm him in them (348d).[7]

We surely do this. We are most in "need" of someone else— neither a companion of use or pleasure—when we least *need* him or her. In other words, the highest things flow out of non-necessity, out of the wonder and freedom of the truth, of *what is*, when we understand it, reflect on it.

I have often remarked to my somewhat dubious students that the pub may be the most important institution on (or more often off) campus. Though I am not opposed to a beer or a good wine, this is not the "metaphysical" purpose of the pub—the late Charles McCabe in San Francisco used to say that a good bar is a place that pours a good drink, a place that lets us talk, even be silent.

I do not mean, of course, that students, professors, and all who presume to think do not need a place just to blow off steam. They need this, surely. But something more profound is at issue here. We need places for conversation, sometimes quiet, sometimes rather raucous. It may be a dinner party at home with friends, a drink in a pub, a walk like those Socrates and Aristotle used to take. But we do need a place just to talk, to be active in the highest sense.

Immediately before the passage from Plato cited above, Socrates had been answering questions Protagoras refused to treat. Socrates, then, asked Hippias, Alcibiades, Protagoras, and Callias to notice that, at ordinary banquets, people chatter about poetry and such "because they are not able to converse with or answer one another while they are drinking, with the sound of their voices and conversation". As a result, they bring on the "flute-girls" and all, for a high price, too. Here is how Socrates continued:

> But where the company are real gentlemen and men of education, you will see no flute-girls, or dancing girls, or harp-girls, and they have no nonsense or games, but are contented with

[7] Plato, *Protagoras*, trans. Jowett-Oswald (New York: Library of the Liberal Arts, 1956), 52.

one another's conversation, of which their own voices are the medium and which they carry on by turns and in an orderly manner, *even though they consume a lot of wine* (347d).[8]

Needless to say, this confirms my thesis on pubs, while today the "dancing girls" are, happily, often quite good conversationalists, reflective of being.

Thus, we actualize ourselves, become what we are, through interpersonal communications in "the order of being". We converse with one another, our friends and companions, not for use or pleasure, but to a higher purpose: to discover and tell one another about the *that which is* we have learned, and to listen to being as experienced by our companions. For these too are personal *I*'s, likewise amazed at the being they did not make, who rush "to confirm" us in its discovery, in freedom and knowing and loving, often in pubs and walks that need not, like creation itself, exist at all.

---

[8] Ibid., 51, italics added.

17

On Cuss-Words

A book any bemused student or other less exalted type from the leisured classes should have on his desk is Fowler's *Modern English Usage*. On the dust jacket of my copy, it says, correctly, that this is a book that "can never be out of date", since Fowler's purpose was "to teach clear thinking and orderly use of precise words and to castigate whatever is slovenly, pretentious, or pedantic".[1] But the trouble with Fowler is that once you get hooked into following its cross-references, it becomes a sort of end in itself, so amusing that you soon forget what it was you started to look for.

I began, for reasons that will become clear later, to look up the word "cuss", but it wasn't in Fowler. Fowler had let me down. I tried to figure out what other word might cover the matter—like invective, swearing, oath, even perhaps humor. Nothing. Then I realized "to cuss", or better "to cuss out", and "you old cuss" are probably "Americanisms" of some sort. I believe Fowler is not terribly amused by said "Americanisms".

So my research led me to "vogue words", which yielded this sound advice:

> The reason for collecting [vogue words] under a common heading is that young writers may not even be aware, about

[1] H. W. Fowler, *A Dictionary of Modern English Usage*, revised by Sir Ernest Gowers (Second Edition; New York: Oxford University Press, 1965), s.v. vogue words.

some of them, that their loose use is corrupting the vocabulary, and that when they are not chosen as significant words but gatecrash as clichés, they are repulsive to the old and well-read.

No one wants to be "repulsive", let alone slovenly or pedantic, right? And with that I figured that maybe cuss-words were not much in vogue in England anyhow.

But since I am an American, I have even seen and heard cuss-words on TV, during that year's St. Louis–Kansas City World Series, in fact. My immediate pursuit of this now-growing problem, however, led me first to Mark Twain. I recalled he had talked about the art of cussing someplace. I paged through my old copy of *Huckleberry Finn*. Sure enough, the raft, with Jim, Huck, the Duke, and the King on it, was preparing to tie up at a little town "well down the State of Arkansaw". Naturally, it was advisable to case the place so the motley crew of the raft could pass as an English Shakespearean Company to do scenes from *Hamlet* and *Richard III*.

Here is how Huck sized up the "Arkansaw" town:

> All the stores was along one street. They had white domestic awning posts. There was empty dry goods boxes under the awnings, and loafers roosting on them all day long, whittling them with their Barlow knives; and chawing tobacco, and gaping and yawning and stretching—a mighty ornery lot. They generally had on yellow straw hats most as wide as an umbrella, but didn't wear no coats or waistcoats; they called one another Bill, and Buck, and Hank, and Joe, and Andy, and talked lazy and drawly, and *used considerable cuss-words* (emphasis added).

The scene was unforgettable, even Fowler would have had to call the words "clear, orderly, and precise", in spite of the raging Americanisms. We do not even need to be told what specific cuss-words Hank and Buck were yelling out at each other in that Arkansaw town—that would be sort of anticlimactic. Our imaginations do a better job.

But, on occasion, we do hear cuss-words—even from the ladies. For those who could read lips, the last game of the 1985 World Series in Kansas City provided an eloquent lesson in cussing when St. Louis manager Whitey Herzog told the plate umpire just what he thought he was. Even though the sound system was not tuned into this memorable scene, those of us learned in linguistics had no trouble at all in figuring out what Herzog had in mind. He was immediately tossed out of the game for cussing the umpire, of course.

The next morning, I inquired of the Elements in Political Theory class, then happily steeped in the *Ethics* of Aristotle, "Why was this baseball scene a lesson in the Aristotelian notion of virtue?" Needless to say, most of the class looked at Schall as if he were fast approaching the fringes, except for those few mad youth who had actually seen the event in Kansas City and were able to read lips. They knew that Aristotle had been on the mark, ancient Greek though he was. They definitely saw exemplified a failure of reason to control emotions.

Moreover, Aristotle had suggested somewhere in Book Four of the *Ethics* that we should pay attention to our language. Indeed, Aristotle told us that controlling our language is rather a minor virtue to enable us to participate in polite social inter-course, well, even to participate in conversation about the highest things. Aristotle mostly wanted us to control, more or less, our anger, so that we do not call umpires and others what we really think they are.

On the other hand, the human animal is so constructed that it often goes beyond what is appropriate. And perhaps particular circumstances might indicate the right time, the right place, at which some umpires deserve a good cussing-out, such that justice would not be done until they got it. Whitey Herzog, recalling the call at first base in the sixth game, might be a rational man after all.

The fine art of cussing, however, can appear in more elegant surroundings, as Fowler's lack of discussion of the subject might suggest. Last year, Michael Jackson gave me a copy of *The World of Wodehouse Clergy*. He gave it to me, I think, because he had spotted tendencies similar to the ones the book describes in one of the clerical members of the Government Department at Georgetown, where Michael had studied.

In a story called " 'Tried in the Furnace': Young Men in Spats", two blades with the unlikely names of Mr. Cyril ("Barmey") Fotheringay-Phipps and Mr. Reginald ("Pongo") Twistleton-Twistleton, were rehearsing for an annual smoking concert at the Drones' Club. While they were at a local grocery store ("The Thorpe and Widgery", to be exact), in came Miss Angelica Briscoe, from the local vicarage in Maiden Eggesford, the daughter of the local clergyman. Well, naturally both gentlemen were smitten by the sight of this lovely young lady, which event caused some friction between these other-wise good friends.

Barmey, it seems, had later managed to meet the charming young Miss Angelica Briscoe, on the occasion of which becoming known to Pongo, the following snippet on our very subject occurred:

> "Have you been sneaking around behind my back and inflicting your beastly society on Miss Briscoe?" he demanded.
>
> "I do not like your tone, Reginald."
>
> "Never mind about my tone. Of all the bally low hounds that ever stepped you are the lowest. So this is what the friend-ship of years amounts to, is it? You crawl in here, and try to cut me out with the girl I love."
>
> "Well, dash it . . . "
>
> "That's quite enough."
>
> "But dash it . . . " [2]

Now, here the "cussing-out" is just as effective with vivid, improbable words like "dash it", or "bally low hounds", "beastly", or "crawl" as with the more well-known cuss-words we read in crummy novels or see on the lips of an annoyed Whitey Herzog, in praise of the plate umpire.

What then, you ask, is the proper use of cuss-words? Well, this whole search began with a letter a friend of mine in San Francisco sent to me·not too long ago. This is a lady with three lively little boys of grammar school vintage, the very

---

2 *The World of Wodehouse Clergy* (London: Hutchinson, 1984), 147.

period of life, if I recall, during which little boys especially
begin to experiment with cussing. This is the record of a conversation with her boys, names of troops not necessarily
altered. I suspect it is a scene most mothers of boys could easily
relate to:

> I must watch myself. Grant [middle boy, maybe seven] said to
> me, "Mom, how come you swear?" (No, he didn't say swear,
> he said, "use so many bad words when you get mad?") At first,
> I decided to cover my maternal image and replied, that "bad
> words released tensions, they come quickly to one's mind in
> the heat of anger . . . " And as his eyes glazed over and he
> stifled a yawn at my explanation, I added, "The truth is, Grant,
> it keeps me from slugging you guys." "Oh", he answered,
> quite attentive again. Of course, one seldom gets angry with
> Grant. Brendan [slightly older brother] did tell me Sunday that
> he "preferred to have *me* mad at him, not Daddy".

That last remark suddenly brought back scenes from my own
youth in Iowa when my brothers and I suddenly froze when
our good father had had it, and he reached for his belt with the
words, "Damn it . . . "

In conclusion, then, I suppose these words of my friend on
the subject of cuss-words are about as "clear-thinking-and-
orderly-use-of-precise-words" as we can arrive at on this topic.
Aristotle was, in the end, quite correct. We learn our earliest
moral concepts in the household—or as Grant put it, on hearing why his dear mother *really* used cuss-words, "Oh!" The
"practical" intellects of the young Grants, Brendans, Joes,
Bucks, Andys, Hanks, Bills, Pongos, and Barmeys of this world
begin to develop, to see *what is*, with such insights, rooted in
their mothers' straight talk and their fathers' reinforcement
potential.

18

A Few Thoughts
about Christmas Reading

After class on the Monday after Thanksgiving, one of my students, Mr. Patrick Kelly, assigned me a short essay, due quite soon, on Christmas Reading. When I was younger in the Order (in the Society of Jesus, that is) we "scholastics", as we were haplessly called in our long years of study, were generally expected to read the work we were assigned in class to do over a semester. This meant, in practice, that our leisure reading— novels and things—was confined to odd half-hours (at the cost of a siesta) or to vacations, to Christmas in particular. I recall with some pleasure going through the library on the Feast of Stephen with two free weeks ahead of me to read whatever I wanted. I habitually checked out thrice as many books as I could possibly read. I have always thought that there was something valuable in just holding a book even if you could not read it.

Not that I did not like reading what was assigned, don't get me wrong. But we had good libraries and wandering through them revealed hundreds of books that somehow just had to be looked at and held. Discovering what we do not know is rather an exhilarating and, at the same time, humbling experience. We tend to specialize too soon. I never read much Jane Austen till I was fifty-seven. I weep, but I am glad I waited too. How could any novel be more wonderful, I asked myself on finishing, than *Persuasion* or *Emma*?

Many of the delightful and profound books I have read were somehow discovered by chance, through no fault of my own. A couple of years ago a friend of mine sent me from England a new paperbound edition from the Oxford University Press of Belloc's *The Four Men*. Maybe there is a more touching and poignant book than this. If so, I have yet to find it. But I never would have read it were it not for my friend's certainty I would like it. It is nice to have friends who know what you like even when you yourself don't. Like life itself, the best things in life are often given to us for no good reason we can figure out at all. Yet these are the things we remember.

So I do not think Christmas reading should be primarily a sort of catch-up period for things that we did not get to during the semester, a kind of extension of class. Forget class during Christmas, but don't forget life and the pleasures of reading. To be sure, I love class, especially when I can assign really wonderful books that anyone in his right mind would want to read, if anyone has a right mind.

A couple of students came up to me the other day to thank me for assigning E. F. Schumacher's *A Guide for the Perplexed*. I was pleased. I really hate to assign a book to students that I am not myself excited about. But there is a certain pleasure in reading something wholly unexpected and unknown to us, something we chance upon because some crotchety old professor like—dare I say it?—Father Schall, in a wild moment, suggested it.

The first thing I am going to recommend is a mystery novel, one I am only half through right now but will have finished in a couple of days, if the wind is with me. It is Dorothy Sayers' *The Nine Tailors*. About a month ago, a friend of mine spotted this book in a secondhand bookstore over in Virginia and gave it to me from out of nowhere.

I was hooked from the first line of the Foreword, which read, "From time to time complaints are made about the ringing of church bells. It seems strange that a generation which tolerates the uproar of the internal combustion engine and the wailing of the jazz band should be so sensitive to the one loud noise that is made to the glory of God." That was originally written in 1934. The motto of the Society of Jesus is "To the Greater Glory of God", and I like jazz bands and church bells. It's providential, right?

The "Nine Taylors" are the rings of a church bell, the Taylor, nine times, to indicate that someone has died. The "Nine Taylors" are followed by one ring for each year of the deceased's life. When they hear the "Nine Taylors", the village counts the single bells to surmise who it is from among them who has died.

I had just been reading Dorothy Sayers' *The Man Born to Be King*, which Ignatius Press had just reissued. This is Miss Sayers' series of radio plays on the life of Christ, done for the BBC during World War II, a most moving and powerful account by Miss Sayers, herself one of the great translators of Dante into English. This is an extraordinarily gripping life of Christ.

Indeed, now that I think of Miss Sayers, for Christmas a couple of years ago (if they don't get books, clerics get sweaters for Christmas), I received the three volumes in the Penguin series of Dante's *Divine Comedy*. I believe Miss Sayers did the "Purgatorio" in that series. Anyhow, on receiving it, I spent the next months reading *The Divine Comedy*. It took me till Easter to finish it. I am still not quite sure anything is so lovely as *The Divine Comedy*. *The Nine Taylors*, in any case, I found to be something difficult to put down. It is a murder mystery. Read it, and do not neglect the metaphysics in it. Wonder why great and sane thinkers like Miss Sayers wrote mystery stories.

So begin with Belloc or Sayers or Dante or Schumacher or Jane Austen. Read them for pleasure, for delight. Why else, ultimately, are we given the highest things?

Next I think a little P. G. Wodehouse would be in order. No one writes better than Wodehouse. Before you start, get a dictionary, because the funniest man who ever wrote in the English language knows it better than you do. You will miss much if you think you know more than Wodehouse about English or about the human condition. What to start with?

Well, really, start with anything. I believe I started with *Right Ho, Jeeves*, which one of my former students, Michael Jackson, gave me. But maybe it was *Leave It to Psmith*. If Wodehouse does not make you glad to be alive, then "abandon all hope", as Dorothy Sayers might have translated Dante.

You will wonder if I am going to suggest anything, well, "intellectual". I already have—novels, mystery stories, travel stories, and Wodehouse are intellectual if there ever was anything of that nature. And you will be amazed at Schumacher. Remember that comedy is more profound than tragedy, and the life of a man on this green earth more touching than the stars and the planets. I can hardly resist suggesting something of Plato. As I did a class on Plato this semester, naturally I am enthusiastic. No one is more surprising than Plato, once you get the hang of him. It took me sixty years to get the hang of him, and I am still working on it. Ask my class.

It is not easy, I know, reading all those dead authors. Like Eric Voegelin, you suspect you ought to read them in the original language. Someone once said that the great majority of the most interesting folks who ever lived are dead. So do not overlook the dead. What about Plato?

Well, I am going to suggest something *about* Plato. It is a wonderful little book that may be difficult to find, but there are libraries even when one lives in Kansas City, and a little investigation into libraries is always worthwhile. This book is Josef Pieper's *Enthusiasm and the Divine Madness*. Isn't that a provoking title? It is about Plato's wonderful dialogue *Phaedrus*. I bought this book someplace once for a couple of dollars. It is one of those rare books about *what is*. Yes, it is all right to read the *Phaedrus* also. You won't believe how good it is.

Finally, I am going to suggest that you ought perhaps to go to the store and buy the latest *Mad Magazine*. You think me daft? mad? I always used to figure that if *Mad* is parodying something in the movies or media, which is their bread and butter, their laughter will indicate where true sanity really lies. You mean that the last thing I am going to recommend is *Mad Magazine*, something the advanced student gave up in grammar school? Well, you probably ran into some good things in grammar school that ought not to be given up, like *Mad*.

I just happen to have an old volume of *Mad* collectabilia. If I were to say it is one of the most profound as well as amusing books I have, you would think I am spoofing you. Well, be spoofed. In it (it bears the title *Greasy Mad Stuff*), there is a section called "The Verse of the People", which begins with this explanation: "Some time ago (*Mad*, no. 43), we dedicated our pages to some brilliant, but unknown, new American poets, in an effort to help these talented young writers get what they deserved. Since then, we have found several more who deserve the same thing." By now, if you have read this far in this essay, you no doubt suspect that you too, like the readers of *Mad*, "get what you deserved"!

The new volume is entitled *The Mad Treasury of Unknown Poetry*, Volume II. I will only cite one stanza of one of the "new" authors who is getting what he deserves, a certain A. E. Housefrau, whose poem is entitled "When I Was a Used Car Salesman". It begins:

> When I was a used car salesman
> I heard the boss–man say,
> "Give free balloons to kiddies
> But not this Ford away!"

Well, you see what I mean? I mean, you won't understand it unless you are semi–literate, and that is a good beginning. Your Introduction to Poetry class comes in handy, and you never thought it would.

Because, after all, I am a clergyman, I think, in conclusion, I should suggest something for the soul. So let me call to your attention a small book that I particularly admire. I guarantee you that it is not like any other pious book you have ever read, if you have read any other books, pious or otherwise. This is a book written on something of a dare in 1908. Someone challenged its author, and he could not resist. You sort of have to admire his spirit. The book—the first chapter is entitled "In

Defense of Everything"—begins: "The only possible excuse for this book is that it is an answer to a challenge. Even a bad shot is dignified when he accepts a duel." It does not take many pages to realize that here we have no bad shot.

You can still get this book in several editions—Doubleday Image has one, Ignatius Press has another, any library has it. This book is G. K. Chesterton's *Orthodoxy*. Don't let the name throw you. It is about the only belief that isn't dull. There is no book quite like this one, unless it is any other book Chesterton wrote. You can read this book in a couple of hours, or a couple of days, or a couple of years, or, like me, all your life. It does not make much difference how often you read it, for it is always a new book.

If you like, you can toss most of your theology and philosophy books away, but you will want to keep this one. You won't forget it even if you think it is blasphemy, which, of course, in a way, it is. I think you need a rather heavy touch of bravery to read this book, for our souls are unprepared to hear what it has to say, which is, I suppose, why I think it something good to read during Christmas. The best things we have we are unprepared for.

I shan't go on. If you can't get to these books during a Christmas vacation, try the Summer, and if you don't make it during the Summer, maybe you will come across them when you are, like me, in your fifties before you really look at Jane Austen. It is all right.

The hero of *The Nine Tailors* is Lord Peter Wimsey. On the way to look at the grave of her mother, in which there was found an extra dead body, which caused the mystery, Wimsey speaks to the young fifteen-year-old daughter, now left an orphan after her parents' deaths:

> "H'm", said Wimsey. "If that's the way your mind works, you'll be a writer one day."
>
> "Do you think so? How funny! That's what I want to be. But why?"
>
> "Because you have the creative imagination, which works outward, till finally you will be able to stand outside your own

experience and see it as something you have made, existing independently of yourself. You're lucky."

"Do you really think so?" Hilary looked excited.

"Yes—but your luck will come more at the end of life than at the beginning, because the other sort of people won't understand the way your mind works. They will start by thinking you dreamy and romantic, and then they'll be surprised to discover that you are really hard and heartless. They'll be quite wrong both times—but they won't ever know it, and you won't know it at first, and it'll worry you."

"But that's just what the girls say at school. How did you know? . . . I thought they're all idiots—mostly, that is."

"Most people are," said Wimsey, gravely, "but it isn't kind of you to tell them. I expect you do tell them so. Have a heart; they can't help it."

So whether we are dreamy or romantic or hard or heartless or idiots or excited because our luck came at the end of our lives rather than at the beginning, the human condition is pretty much as Lord Peter Wimsey, at the end, said it was. We will find it is so, particularly if we remember the divine comedy in which we were given life but, yes, only if we accept its challenge, only if we choose it.

Mad Magazine sought to help the unknown poets "get what they deserved". We won't get what we deserve, but far more. This is the suspicion you will get if you take a look at any of the books I have rashly suggested you waste your Christmas vacation on. Or as it says in *Leave It to Psmith*, "It is the opinion of the most thoughtful students of life that happiness in this world depends chiefly on the ability to take things as they come." In the end, that is what you should ponder during Christmas vacation in the things you read, the problem about the meaning of "happiness in this world" and whether it has anything to do with Christmas itself.

19

Worthless Except for Baptizing

John Paul I, it happily turned out, was not merely Pope for thirty-three days. He also wrote a lovely book called *Illustrissimi*.[1] I had prodded a friend of mine to locate a copy of this wonderful book, so I now have it. John Paul I's "Letters to Famous People" are simply endearing. No Christian, practicing or otherwise engaged, should fail to read them.

Here, I want to comment only on his "Letter to Mark Twain", as Twain comes up several times in these essays. "You were one of my favorite authors during my adolescence", Albino Luciani (John Paul I's given name) began. He fondly recalled Tom Sawyer, as all of us Americans surely do also. He admitted to telling hundreds of Mark Twain stories. His favorite was one about books—whose value varied, according to Twain, "beyond calculation".

For example, some leather-bound books were good for sharpening razors; small books good for wedging under table legs, French books were especially good for this propping. Thick books like dictionaries were useful for throwing at noisy cats, and atlases were quite helpful in keeping windowpanes from rattling. The Pope revealed that, when he was a teacher, his pupils were delighted when he would announce, "Now I will tell you another Mark Twain story."

But he confesses that the members of his diocese were shocked—a bishop quoting Mark Twain, somewhat of an

[1] John Paul I, *Illustrissimi* (Boston: Little Brown, 1978).

agnostic! The letter went on to recall Twain's remark that there were three persons in each of us, not exactly a trinity, but the man each thinks he is, the man others think he is, and the man he really is.

Well, I figure that if a pope can recall Mark Twain, likewise can I, though it does seem sobering that the last Italian Pope spent his youth happily reading more of Twain than most of us Americans do. Twain in his *Life on the Mississippi*—it is written under his real name, Samuel Clemens—told of leaving St. Louis on a riverboat while reflecting how much things had changed since he was a boy on the river.

Twain returned to his stateroom to find a young man called Rogers, crying. "Rogers was not his name; neither was Jones, Brown, Dexter, Ferguson, Bascom, nor Thompson, but he answered to either of these . . . or to any other name, in fact, if he perceived that you meant him."

And why was Rogers, Jones, Brown, Dexter, Ferguson, Bascom, or Thompson crying? Well, he just wanted to have a drink of water, and all there was about was Mississippi River "slush".

Twain: "Can't you drink it?"

Rogers, Jones, Brown, etc: "I could if I had some other water to wash it down with."

Mark Twain then reflected that at least the water was the same, muddy. Every tumblerful would still hold "nearly an acre of land in solution".

Just as in Genesis, the land and sea could be separated if you let the tumbler sit for an hour. Furthermore, you could drink the solution. Natives just gulped down the gruel-like water with pleasure. Strangers, Twain said, were not used to it, but when they were, they preferred river water to *real* water.

Twain concluded: "This was really the case. It is good for steamboating, and good to drink; but *it is worthless for all other cases, except baptizing*" (emphasis added).

Now, I do not know whether Albino Luciani ever told his good pupils this delightful story of Twain's. However, the Rogers, Jones, Brown, Dexter, Ferguson, Bascom, Thompson character might prove there are more than three persons in each of us! But which one do we baptize, even with Mississippi River water? The one others think we are? The one we think we are? The one we really are?

Albino Luciani's conclusion was one that the American humorist probably would not himself have drawn. "But, I who am a bishop must; and I urge my faithful: If you happen to think of the three Johns, the three James, the three Francises that are in each of us, pay special attention to the third: the one whom God likes."

Baptize that one with Mississippi River water . . . !

Yes, just as there are various kinds of books, so there are various kinds of bishops. Sometimes, the latter become popes. Do not miss *Illustrissimi*—and when you have finished with your copy, I am sure neither Mark Twain nor Albino Luciani would mind if you were to use it to sharpen your razor, or prop up the table leg, or quiet rattling windows, or best, throw at howling cats.

Probably, though, I will keep the copy of *Illustrissimi* that I have. No cat is worth the most charming book I have read in a long time. And if you—Rogers, Jones, Brown, Dexter, Ferguson, Bascom, Thompson, John, James, Francis, I, II, or III— ever wondered about the papacy before Albino Luciani and Mark Twain, I am sure, on finishing *Illustrissimi*, you will think it an even greater, more wonderful mystery—you, whoever you think you are, whoever others think you are, or whoever God thinks you are.

20

The Truest Philosophy

My brother-in-law has a collection of Gilbert and Sullivan records. While I was visiting him this Summer, I listened to the *Yeoman of the Guard*, which had a printed libretto with it. In Act I, I came across the following passage of Jack Point's:

> My masters, I pray you bear with us, and we will satisfy you, for we are merry folk who would make all as merry as ourselves. For, look you, there is humour in all things, and the truest philosophy is that which teaches us to find it and to make the most of it.

My sister, who plays the piano and sings quite well, fortunately did not ask me to sing this for her, but it remains, in my mind, a remarkable passage—the search for the "truest philosophy".

That humor is more metaphysical than tragedy, I have never had any doubt. Those are not perceptive who bitterly complain against the existence of the Deity on the grounds that he allows sorrow and evil in the world. The real problem, as Jack Point hinted, is that he allows laughter. And the proper word is, indeed, "allows", every bit as much as "allow" in the case of evil and sorrow. For laughter, if it be not ours, cannot be at all.

It is a commonplace that few great philosophers ever treated well the topic of laughter. Bergson had something on it, I believe; and, of course, Aristotle defined us as beings who "laugh", or maybe he meant "beings who are funny". How often, in fact, have we been where something is funny and nobody laughed?

However, Jack Point, in the *Yoeman of the Guard*, actually said that the "truest philosophy" was not so much humor as that philosophy that teaches us to find it. A couple of years ago in a used-book store on Clement Street in San Francisco, I bought a 1946 edition of Louis Untermeyer's *A Treasury of Laughter*. I think I paid a dollar for it.

In it, there was a card that read, "Dear Reader, It's a great pleasure to send you the accompanying volume, as a book-dividend, to which you are entitled by reason of your recent purchases of two Book-of-the-Month Club selections. We hope that you and your family will enjoy it. (Signed) Harry Sherman, President." It seems a pity not to thank Harry Sherman for this little gift, even though it was not meant for me. The original owner left no mark in this book, which makes me wonder whether anyone ever read it before. Somehow, I like used books with signs in them that somebody has previously read them, if only a penciled-in "nonsense" after some profound passage.

In his introduction, Untermeyer wrote that "few books point out that man's way of laughing, as well as his reasons for laughter, change from generation to generation. The very word 'humor' has meant different things to different centuries. In the sixteenth century, for example, the prime meaning of humor was 'a disorder of the blood'; the Greeks, according to Hippocrates, believed the human body contained four 'humors': namely, blood, phlegm, yellow bile, and black bile." Perhaps some Greek, like Aristotle, explained how we got from yellow bile to Bob Hope.

One of the selections in the book was from Finley Peter Dunne, called "Alcohol as Food". Mr. Dooley, in response to Hennessey's argument that alcohol was indeed food, put it this way, with benefit of clergy:

> "No whisky ain't food. I think better iv it thin that. I wudden't insult it be placin' it on th' same low plane as a lobster salad. Father Kelly puts it r-right, and years go by without him

lookin' on it even at Hallowe'en. 'Whisky', he says, 'is called th' divvle, because', he says, ' 'tis wan iv th' fallen angels', he says. 'It ought to be th' reward iv action, not th' cause iv it', he says. 'It's f'r the end iv th' day, not th' beginnin',' he says. 'Hot whisky is good f'r a cold heart, an' no whisky's good f'r a hot head', he says." [1]

I had never realized that whiskey was one of the "fallen angels", but you learn something new every day. And the notion that whiskey ought to be the reward of action, not the cause of it, is mindful of Chesterton's remark that we should thank the Lord for good red wine by not drinking too much of it.

But this is a metaphysical comment, not one on temperance, though there is something metaphysical about moderation too. The truest philosophy—this involves an understanding of the world in which there is abundance, freedom, risk, vice, endings, and beginnings.

> There was a young lady from Guam
> Who observed, "The Pacific's so calm
> That there can't be a shark.
> I'll just swim for a lark."
>
> . . . .
>
> Let's now sing the Twenty-Third Psalm.

Whiskey, the divvle, the lady from Guam, black bile, The Lord Is My Shepherd—for we are merry folk who would make all as merry as ourselves. From cold hearts and hot heads, deliver us, O Lord.

[1] Finley Peter Dunne, "Alcohol as Food", in *A Treasury of Laughter*, ed. Louis Untermeyer (New York: Simon and Schuster, 1946), 217.

21

On Fellowship and the "Baby Jesus"

Christmas of 1983, I celebrated Midnight Mass at the lovely Poor Clares' Convent in Aptos, California, with an old friend from the University of Santa Clara, Father Edward Warren, S.J. This convent is in the parish to which my brother Jerry and his dear family belong, so we usually attend Christmas Mass either at Resurrection Parish across California Highway One or at the Poor Clares', though we normally have Sunday Mass when I am about at nearby Villa Maria del Mar Chapel of the Holy Names Sisters. This old wooden chapel above the cliffs at Santa Cruz, where one can often hear the waves crashing below during Mass, is a favorite of the family, I think.

At the Poor Clares', the Sister Sacristan had carefully instructed us about the entrance ceremony for the Midnight Mass. The sisters in choir would be singing carols, always a touching and beautiful moment, while we would proceed from the back of the chapel. Father Warren was the principal celebrant.

On the way into the sanctuary before the crowded congregation, we were to stop briefly to incense the Christmas crib, with its manger, animals, shepherds, and angels singing on high. I was to carry on a cushion a "Baby Jesus" doll in the procession and place it in the crib just before the incensing. The scene, I realized, was fraught with unaccustomed danger, as I knew my brother and nephews would be carefully watching how Uncle Jim, a liturgical clubfoot, would handle this delicate role.

Sure enough, when we got into the sanctuary, with the lights appropriately lowered, the firs, greenery, and poinsettias all about, I panicked, as I had not noticed ahead of time just where the said crib might be. As lead man, I could not figure out where I was supposed to put the "Baby Jesus". Everything seemed alike to me, so I saw on my left something that looked like perhaps an advanced-design crib and walked over to it. But this turned out to be the lectern or sanctuary-lamp stand. I was frozen.

Meanwhile, Father Warren, with the incense, and the altar boys had turned right, while Uncle Jim was wandering around the santuary-lamp stand looking for a crib in which to put the "Baby Jesus" doll down. When someone finally hissed, I looked around to see Father Warren calmly over at the crib, waiting for me to get my bearings. I began to giggle at this preposterous Christmas scene in which Uncle Jim could not even find the crib, let alone the inn or the manger.

Needless to say, my brother and nephews were merciless when it was all finally over, though the dear nuns, who must have been collapsing in their secluded choir, and my nieces and sister-in-law were charmingly delicate about the whole scene. My nephews, I fear, have offered to buy me a leash the next Christmas I will appear at the Poor Clares' Convent Chapel. I am sure, theologically, the real Baby Jesus understands.

On December 31, 1963, just a few months before she died, Flannery O'Connor wrote that her lupus had put her into bed, causing her to miss Christmas Mass. But she did hear of the participation of her pet burro at the local Milledgeville, Georgia, religious Christmas pageants.

> Ernest—that is Equinox' pa—did the honors for the burros this Christmas and went both to the Christian manger and the Methodist pageant. He did very well in the Christian manger—in which there were also a cow, a pig, a shetland pony & some sheep and he did all right at the Methodist dress rehearsal

but when the big moment came and the church full of Methodists, he wouldn't put a foot inside the door. Doesn't care for "fellowship" I suppose.[1]

Burros in Georgia who don't care for "fellowship", clergy in Aptos who cannot find the crib—of such is Christmas. Somehow there is a profound connection, often illustrated by the Christmas mysteries, between solemnity and humor. Indeed, I suspect, the connection is ultimately metaphysical and more.

In an earlier letter (June 19, 1957), Flannery O'Connor had been asked about the origin of some of her most "grotesque" and unusual characters. She responded that her "standard of judgment" could only arise within Christianity, "because it concerns specifically Christ and the Incarnation, the fact that there has been a unique intervention in history. It's not a matter in these stories of Do unto Others. That can be found in any ethical culture series. It is the fact of the Word made flesh." [2]

What this suggests at Christmas is that the particular mode of revelation—God becoming a child—is precisely "grotesque", as Flannery O'Connor put it, because it is the least likely mode of redemption that the human mind, as such, could imagine. There is a kind of "death-wish" in humanity, as the Russian scientist, Igor Shafarevich put it, that cannot accept the goodness of what we are and what God is, of God's way of doing things.

This too is why the "political messianisms" that charge so much of our public life today, even in religion itself, are at pains to stress the "Do unto Others" as the primary mode of redemption. For them, the Incarnation is a scandal, as it must be to all self-redeeming religions or philosophies. Uncle Jim wandering confusedly about a sanctuary looking for a crib, or the burro Ernest, "Equinox' pa", refusing to have "fellowship" with the Methodists on Christmas Eve, is far closer to the par-

[1] Flannery O'Connor, *The Habit of Being: The Letters of Flannery O'Connor* (New York: Vintage, 1979), 555.
[2] Ibid., 227.

ticular reality of our being than learned dissertations and vio-
lent movements to save all mankind from sundry "exploi-
tations".

The Second Reading for the Dawn Mass at Christmas is
from Saint Paul's Epistle to Titus: "But when the kindness and
love of God our Savior for mankind were revealed, it was not
because he was concerned with any righteous actions we might
have done ourselves; it was for no reason except his own compassion that he saved us." Compared to this salvation, the only
one there is, all else will seem odd or strange, particularly those
"salvations" we dream up ourselves.

But immersed in the mysteries of the Incarnation, of the
Word made flesh, we discover both the solemnity and the
humor, because we are indeed freed from the burden of saving
ourselves. Something greater has already been given to us, and
we can hardly name it. In being given more than we could
have hoped, we find our own hopes paltry before the destiny
to which we are actually called. And this is our joy, liturgical
clubfeet though we be. The Incarnation is not what we would
have expected, but it is what we got. Rejoice and be glad!

22

The Routine for Joining a Monastery

Somehow these days, my students have begun to assign me, their academic mentor, things to do. Definitely this reflects a basic disorder in the universe. Not infrequently, students have the uncanny capacity to teach their professors a thing or two. Fortunately, they do not charge Ivy League tuition. What was it Holden Caulfield said in *Catcher in the Rye*? "You don't have to think too hard when you talk to a teacher."

Anyhow, that is how I came to read Jay McInerney's *Bright Lights, Big City* and Bret Easton Ellis' *Less than Zero*. The first is about a distraught young man working in a New York publishing house for a boss named Clara Tillinghast, or "The Clinger", who "has a mind like a steel mousetrap and a heart like a twelve-minute egg". The second novel is about a young man's Christmas vacation in Los Angeles from a college in New Hampshire. Close to the heart, these. Henry Walker, one of my students, had read these first novels and had also seen a column in which George Will compared them (mostly unfavorably) with J. D. Salinger's first novel, *Catcher in the Rye*, of some thirty years ago. Thus, we have here sort of comparative stuff: decline and fall, savored corruption.

I read *Bright Lights* on the way down to Houston for a conference one Winter, *Less than Zero* on the return flight to Washington, D.C. In Houston, the young college graduates, Fighting Irish types from Notre Dame (my cousin's dear young daughter included), were all either into space (they worked for

NASA) or into Saint Thomas at the Basilian Fathers' university there.

On finishing these novels, I thought that the student who gave them to me was quaintly trying to be sure Schall was acquainted with the drug culture. At least that seemed to be the main activity of the young folks in the two first novels. Sort of sad, definitely boring. Holden Caulfield drank once in a while, but he seemed to be bothered mostly by existence itself, not unfavorably, which takes a lot of insight, as old Phoebe, Caulfield's dear little sister, taught him.

Ellis, in fact, seems to have discovered and described Augustine's City of Man right there in Los Angeles. Others, needless to say, have found it there before him. After the young hero Clay finally got through Christmas vacation, no mean feat in a plot that seemed to have been concocted from the pages of an old moral theology casebook of exotic aberrations, he set down this anti-city, anti-civilizational theme, rather Rousseau-like:

> The images I had were of people being driven mad by living in the city. Images of parents who were so hungry and unfulfilled that they ate their own children. Images stayed with me even after I left the city. Images so violent and malicious that they seemed to be my only point of reference for a long time afterwards. After I left.[1]

I am not sure, in retrospect, if college back in New Hampshire turned out to have been more wholesome than L.A. (I happen to like L.A. in fact), but the images of "people being driven mad by living in the city" deserve to be contrasted with Augustine's own experience as a young man living in the L.A. of his day—Rome itself, where I spent so many years.

Augustine seems to have duplicated most of the L.A. (and New York) feats, but you have to admit *The Confessions* not only make better reading, but Augustine had a lot more ideas, even more flaky ones, not to mention the sane ones. Try to be

---

[1] Bret Easton Ellis, *Less Than Zero* (Baltimore: Penguin, 1987).

a Manichee, for instance, or a Pelagian. Well, maybe you have, and just don't know it.

Augustine, in the end, never blamed the city—Rome, L.A.—for what he did himself. Indeed, for Augustine, if the city was disordered, it was largely because Augustine's own heart, over which he had some control if he wanted to exercise it, was disordered. *Less than Zero* struck me as a kind of unredeemed hopelessness, a world with no openings. The all-pervasive dope and everything that went with it seemed to be consequences. However, hell remains what we choose. If the parents "were so hungry and unfulfilled that they ate their own children", the children showed no sign of that inner life into which a spark of grace, let alone will, might fall. Besides, I am tired of kids' blaming their folks for everything wrong with them. Kids, even college kids, have free will too.

I was also given a copy of *Catcher in the Rye*, which I had not read in years. I finished it in Indianapolis, of all places. The most striking difference between these novels is that there is nothing at all funny in *Less than Zero* (you need rationality to have wit, as Aristotle said), perhaps a faint smile now and then in *Bright Lights* [2] (Tobias Wolff, whoever he is, said on the back cover, however, that this book is "smart, heartfelt, and very, very funny"), while *Catcher in the Rye* was full of amusement on practically every page, full of tenderness too.

If you want to get heavy into metaphysics, could I surmise, on the basis of these representative texts, that our culture has lost its laughter and its gentility in these decades? Well, there were some touching passages in *Bright Lights*, especially about the death of the narrator's mother, so all was not lost.

Plato talked of order in the polity reflecting order (or disorder) in the soul—sort of George Will's statecraft and soulcraft. Early in *Bright Lights*, "you" says to himself, "Your soul is as disheveled as your apartment, and until you clean it up a little, you don't want to invite anybody inside." [3] Now, that is rather good advice. Actually, again recalling Augustine, there is noth-

[2] Jay McInerny, *Bright Lights, Big City* (New York: Vintage, 1984).
[3] Ibid., 32.

ing particularly wrong with detailing our disordered souls, but this is done best, as McInerney hinted, after we clean up our own act a bit.

In *Bright Lights*, a redemptive spirit is found. It is concerned with concreteness and the smell of bread even. "You get down on your knees and tear open the bag. The smell of warm dough envelops you. You will have to go slowly. You will have to learn everything all over again." [4] This was the young man's response to his mother's death, in his present state, after he remembered she had asked him about the moral theology lists. "After her funeral, it seemed as if you were wandering around your own interior looking for signs of life, finding nothing but empty rooms and white walls." Void replaced disorder.

In *Catcher in the Rye*, on the other hand, the ultimate act of generosity (lots of acts of generosity in this book) is catching the little children who are playing in the rye fields as they fall accidentally over a cliff, as if there is indeed some providence for all of us. Holden Caulfield seemed more in touch with a tradition—he read books and prayed, sort of.

> I read a lot of classical books, like *Return of the Native*, and all, and I like them . . . What really knocks me out is a book that, when you're all done reading it, you wish the author that wrote it was a terrific friend of yours and you could call him up on the phone whenever you felt like it. That don't happen much, though. I wouldn't mind calling Isak Dinesen up.[5]

Leo Strauss said that the only way you can call Plato or Aristotle or Augustine up is by carefully reading their books.

Here is how Holden prayed, or tried to, though he should have paid more attention to *The Confessions*, as young men easily embrace dubious ideas to explain their dubious behavior.

> I felt like praying or something, when I was in bed, but I couldn't do it. I can't always pray when I feel like it. In the first

[4] Ibid., 182.
[5] J. D. Salinger, *Catcher in the Rye* (Boston: Little Brown, 1951), 25.

place, I'm sort of an atheist. I like Jesus and all, but I don't care too much for most of the other stuff in the Bible. Take the Disciples, for instance. They annoy the hell out of me, if you want to know the truth. They were all right after Jesus was dead, but while he was alive, they were about as much use to Him as a hole in the head. All they did was keep letting Him down.[6]

Holden, the "sort of atheist", thus turned out to be also "sort of a Pelagian", who thought the fact that we let the Lord down is *not* the reason he came in the first place. Augustine had said something about that too. That is why young men and women should read Augustine, for most of the important stuff occurred to him.

In conclusion, there is the zonked-out life of *Less than Zero*, the boring copy room of *Bright Lights*, with its hint of Bread, and Holden, who once thought of being a monk, if you can imagine. Holden woke up old Ackley, his roommate at school:

> "Hey, Ackley . . . Listen. What's the routine for joining a monastery?" I asked him. I was sort of toying with the idea of joining one. "Do you have to be a Catholic and all?"
>
> "Certainly you have to be a Catholic; you bastard, did you wake me up just to ask me a dumb ques . . . "
>
> "Aah, go back to sleep. I'm not gonna join one anyway. The kind of luck I have, I'd probably join one with all the wrong kind of monks in it. All stupid bastards. Or just bastards."[7]

So there you are, in L.A., in college in New Hampshire, in a New York office, Rome, or some godam monastery reading *Return of the Native*. You take your chances, don't you?

But this is what it is all about, really. You take a chance, like the Lord with his Disciples. That means you can let yourself become a little less than zero, or join some monastery full of stupid bastards, meet old Phoebe, or be there when your mother dies, as Augustine also was. They still look for the City of God in Babylon, I notice, even if you call it L.A. or New

[6] Ibid., 130.
[7] Ibid., 65.

23

Gratitude

After he referred to Saint Francis of Assisi and Social Darwinism in his eloquent address to the 1984 Democratic Convention in San Francisco, New York Governor Mario Cuomo was briefly interviewed by Larry King on KCBS. King remarked on the reference to Saint Francis of Assisi. Cuomo went on to cite G. K. Chesterton's comment that Saint Francis may have been the only real democrat who ever lived.

Needless to say, Cuomo never could have been elected if that were true, but I am prejudiced in favor of anyone who knows about Chesterton, though I wish that Mario Cuomo would have also paid attention to what Chesterton said about human life.[1] This reference of Governor Cuomo's reminded me that I had not read Chesterton's *St. Francis of Assisi* for some time. Eventually, in the library of Xavier Hall at the University of San Francisco, I found a 1944 edition of this wonderful book, originally written in 1924.

Everyone, no doubt, has his favorite theme in Chesterton, who remains one of the most quoted authors in the English language. My own favorite, I think, is Chesterton's explanation of the virtue of gratitude. Indeed, I would suspect that gratefulness is the single most revealing element in a man's character. Like anything else, to be sure, gratitude can be corrupted into

[1] See James V. Schall, "The Rarest of All Resolutions: G. K. Chesterton on the Relation of Human Life to Christian Doctrine", *American Benedictine Review*, 32 (December 1981), 304–27.

some sort of fawning or into a kind of lethargic inertness. But in itself, it reveals how we understand the world and our presence in it.

The first step in understanding gratitude is the simple realization that there is something beyond everything, something over which we have no control, but to which we respond as an existence given to us. "The mystic who passes through the moment when there is nothing but God does in some sense behold the beginningless beginnings in which there was really nothing else", Chesterton wrote. "He not only appreciates everything but the nothing of which everything is made."

What does it mean, we might ask, to appreciate "nothing"? The mystic, in Chesterton's view, will be fully aware that all else but God is unnecessary. If anything but God exists, it does so because of something in God and not something in itself. This means that intelligent beings who know what they are can choose to reject what they are, can choose to build their own worlds. This is what used to be called "pride" in the old spiritual books. There is no reason why it should not still be.

The opposite of pride was the choice to accept the fact that reality, including oneself, was more wondrous than we ourselves could have imagined. Chesterton put it this way: The "sense of the great gratitude and the sublime dependence was not a phrase or even a sentiment; it is the whole point that this was at the very rock of reality. It was not a fancy but a fact; rather it is true that beside it all facts are fancies." There are things that need not exist but do exist because of what God is like. Creation, as the medievals said, is the vestige of God; we humans are not gods, but we are his images.

And this was the basis of that courtesy, that democracy, that Chesterton saw in Saint Francis. "What distinguishes this very genuine democrat from any mere demagogue is that he never either deceived or was deceived by the illusion of mass-suggestion. Whatever his [Saint Francis'] taste in monsters, he never saw before him a many-headed beast. He only saw the image of God multiplied but never monotonous." This is, of course, the reality the politician in particular is most likely to forget, the reality of the particular life in all its forms. The unique variety of each of our own kind cannot be exhausted in, or even comprehended by, the political community.

Aristotle, to be sure, understood this when he discussed friendship. This is how Chesterton put it:

> There never was a man who looked into those burning brown eyes without being certain that Francis Bernadone was really interested in him; in his own inner individual life from the cradle to the grave; that he himself was being valued and taken seriously, and not merely added to the spoils of some social policy or the names in some clerical document. Now for this particular moral and religious idea there was no external expression except courtesy.[2]

Courtesy, of course, is our response, at its best, to what others are. It is a sign of our gratitude, not merely for our own existence, but more especially for that of others, whom we could not, by ourselves, imagine ahead of time, yet who exist.

One of the more obvious solutions to the problem of evil is to conceive a world in which no finite, free, intelligent beings could exist. This, presumably, would save us the embarrassment of having a God who "allowed" evil. But we have a God who did not listen to our logic.

The great temptations, they say, are moral. I suspect, however, that they are also metaphysical. A world in which no gratitude existed would be necessarily a world in which our kind could not exist. And this is strange, that the closer we arrive to pride, the closer we arrive to a world in which gratitude does not exist, only our own definition of how the world ought to be, but is not.

Not everyone ought to be a friar or a monk, whatever be the procedures for joining a monastery. Yet the world should contain not a few monks and friars. Of the controversy about whether Franciscans ought to own property, Chesterton wrote:

[2] G. K. Chesterton, *St. Francis of Assisi* (London: Hodder and Stoughton, 1964), 114–15.

Saints were sometimes great men when the Popes were small men. But it also shows, that great men are sometimes wrong when small men are right. And it will be found, after all, very difficult for any candid and clear-headed outsider to deny that the Pope was right, when he insisted that the world was not made only for Franciscans.[3]

That there are many different ways to God seems commonplace. What is not commonplace is the way each of us reaches God. The gift of gratitude includes the fact that God's ways are not our ways, for our ways lead only to ourselves, and we are not God. This latter truth, obvious as it is, again, is why we can be ultimately grateful.

[3] Ibid., 79.

24

Spirituality and Sports

On Opening Day at the San Francisco Giants' Candlestick Park in 1984, some kind soul had put on the Xavier Hall bulletin board at the University of San Francisco, where I was at the time, a five-dollar bleacher ticket—Section 54, Row 14, Seat 1—five seats from being out of the stadium, in other words. But the difference between being in and being out of the stadium is almost mystical. So, contemplating the free ticket, I said to myself, "Schall, you know opening day at the ballpark is a national event, and you have been around on this earth, lo, all these years, and you have never been to an Opening Day. Time is short and besides, Washington, where you usually live, has no 'Senators' anymore." So with this impeccable logic, I went.

The afternoon was very warm, even hot, in San Francisco, in what can be the coldest ballpark in the big leagues. The Cubs were in town for the opener. Fifty-four thousand fans showed up. Four young men sat next to me in Section 54, Row 14. One politely apologized to me in advance for being a loud Cubs fan; and, as the game proceeded, he was funny enough to hold the myriads of Giants rooters at bay, especially as the Cubs won 5–3.

Baseball has its own language—without which you can probably not understand this country. "You're blind, ump!" "Take a walk, McMaster." And at $1.75 a cold bottle, I estimate that enough Millers were sold that afternoon to float a navy destroyer at dry dock in nearby Hunter's Point.

Often, I think, ascetic types argue that spirituality and sports are opposed to each other. Yet when you are around 54,000 cheering, yelling fans at Candlestick, or even watch on TV a championship basketball or football game, with most of the rest of the country, you begin to suspect that something very close to the human spirit is going on down there on the fields and up there in the stands.

At every ball game, something final is decided. Watching, we begin to wonder whether perhaps this is not an image of our own lives, which exist so that we may decide something, something important, something final. There is something human about it all. What was it that John Thompson, the Georgetown University basketball coach, said somewhat irately? "The press can do more than God if you listen to them. I've heard inarticulate people talk to the press for years and they even became articulate." [1]

Sports have to do with being good and with praising what is good because it is good in its own order. Sports fans know their heroes are not "gods", in spite of what the press thinks of itself. But sports fans know that the players are heroes in a way. Sports betray corruption at times, too, no doubt of it. Indeed, the corruption of sports by money or crime or dope seems especially awful because the delicate life of sports need not be at all.

I take it for granted that not a little of an average man's (and woman's) life will be taken up with watching, beer in hand, a ball game of some sort, or with memories of playing in some game or other. This is, to my mind, not a sign of the fall of civilization, though it is possible to fiddle or watch gladiators while Rome burns. The question, of course, is this: what lies behind this natural fascination with sports? What does it have to do, if anything, with the meaning of our existence and our relationship with God?

I cannot imagine that the Cubs rooter next to me at Candlestick Park on Opening Day, 1984, while drinking five Millers,

---

[1] *San Francisco Chronicle*, April 2, 1984.

was particularly worried about such a query. Nevertheless, this game was for him and his friends worth coming to, watching, cheering at, laughing at, and agonizing over when his team was behind. It was worth doing on an April afternoon. At least one thing in the lives of such fans was worth doing just because it was there, for its own sake. They were not going to "get" anything out of it except perhaps a sunburn in the hot sun of a lovely Spring day, or maybe a slight hangover from the beer.

Just as our normal spirituality should attend to natural things, like the rain, sports, for many people, perhaps for most normal folk, should be a part of their spirituality also. We Americans may prefer baseball or football, while most of the world watches soccer, and there is everything from tennis to swimming.

Jim Kline and I, for instance, a few days later, went over to Buck Shaw Stadium to watch the Santa Clara Broncos play Cal Poly in baseball. On the very next field, you could also watch Santa Clara play Cal-Berkeley in lacrosse. All of these sports demand that we expend energy and mind to play well. They present us with something fascinating that need not be at all. And they are worth doing even if we are not the best, though we want to watch someone play "the best", even if we play as if we have two left feet. We could, perhaps, have a world in which there were no sports, but that would demand a creation not made in the "superabundance" of which Aquinas often spoke.

No one, of course, denies that sports playing or watching can be abused, like any other human thing. But the biggest "abuse" of sports is probably the attitude that they are mere frivolities having nothing to do with the meaning and dignity of our lives. There are, no doubt, "higher" things than sports. Yet, these higher things are somehow like sports. Aristotle knew this. Sports hint obscurely at the relation of creation to God and of God to creation.[2]

_____

[2] See James V. Schall, *Far Too Easily Pleased: A Theology of Contemplation, Play, and Festivity* (Los Angeles: Benziger-Macmillan, 1976); "The Law of Superabundance", *Gregorianum*, 72, no. 3 (1991), 515–42.

Ultimately, we may "need" God, but I suspect, when the chips are down (another image from a kind of sport), when we are "face-to-face", as Saint Paul said, we will discover, to our surprise, that the fascination of God is closer to our fascination with our games than almost anything else, except to our friendships and our conversations, both of which spill over into what we do together and talk about. I remain one of those who read the "Green Sheet", the sports page, first. I make no apology. It is an act of spirituality looking obscurely for the highest fascination of *what is*.

25

Rain

In *The Wasteland*, T. S. Eliot wrote:

> There is not even silence in the mountain,
> But dry, sterile thunder without rain.

Where we live, in large part, influences profoundly how we look at the natural phenomena that are so much an often unnoticed part of our daily lives—such things as wind, rain, floods, mountains, seashores, creeks, and plains.

One of my very earliest memories was at my Uncle Tom Hart's farm near Havelock, Iowa. Close by the house on farms in those days was a large earthen cellar, which served to store fruits and vegetables in the days before the refrigerator. But this cellar doubled as a refuge from tornadoes, or cyclones, as we used to call them in Iowa. I can still recall the hush that suddenly came about the barn and the fields; the sky suddenly, ominously darkening; the order from Aunt Margaret for us kids to get into the cellar, because Uncle Tom had seen a funnel dropping down in the distant sky. Then, suddenly, sheets of rain would hit the farm.

The Old Testament, written in a normally parched area, is full of grateful references to rain, while the Gospel of Saint Matthew recalls our Lord's words that the rain, however romantic or annoying, Singin' in the Rain or Tramping through Georgia, falls equally on the just and the unjust. Psalm

147 tells us to "sing to Yahweh in gratitude, play the lyre for our God, who covers the heavens with clouds, to provide the earth with rain, to produce fresh grass on the hillsides and plants that are needed by men." That "fresh grass on the hillsides" always reminds me of the Winter and Spring green on California's Mount Hamilton Range, so brown and purple during the dry months in San Jose.

Saint Paul, stopping over on Malta, was rather less rhapsodic about the rain: "The inhabitants treated us with unusual kindness. They made us all welcome, and they lit a huge fire, because it started to rain and the weather was cold." I never recollect being colder than in Naples or Palermo, not too far from Malta, during the early Spring rains, so I can appreciate what Saint Paul meant by the comfort of a huge fire.

No doubt, it is true that our interior life has mostly to do with our relationship to our family, our friends, and neighbors, to our self-control, to our awareness of them. Saint Francis of Assisi seems to be the saint of nature—I remember being very cold and wet in Assisi also—but more of birds and animals. Yet I think the Gospels are right to tell us to "see the lilies of the field, how they grow", and my Uncle Tom would have liked what Saint James said of the farmer, "how patiently he waits for the precious fruits of the ground until it has had the Autumn rain and the Spring rain".

Both Augustine and Aquinas, in dealing with our very earliest acts, hint that how we see things, often, depends on us. If we think we are imprisoned in a niggardly planet, or cheated by our native turf, we are most likely annoyed by others who have discovered the kingdom of God beginning in these same places. I am, myself, probably more sympathetic to rain and snow than I am to dogs that bite (specifically, me), yet, as I watched my nephew's little Golden Retriever (née: Nutmeg) rush playfully all over the cliffs, sniffing above the beautiful green ice plant, with the sand and the Pacific waves breaking below at Montara and Moss Landing, I knew that the Book of Genesis and Aristotle were right about the orders of creation. Things fit.

To me, the Prologue to the Gospel of Saint John remains the center of our spiritual understanding of nature—of its elements, that all is reflective in its own way of the Word in which all things were created in the first place. We need not, I suppose, rush out into every thunderstorm declaring, at 37th and O Street, just outside the gates at Georgetown, the praise of the Lord just because it is sprinkling. Yet we are somehow dull if the thought never occurs to us.

In Isaiah we read: "Yes, as the rain and the snow come down from the heavens and do not return without watering the earth, making it yield and giving growth to provide seed for the sower and bread for the eating, so the word that goes from my mouth does not return to me empty without carrying out my will, and succeeding in what it was sent to do" (55:10).

The corners of this Green Earth, in which it rains or snows, in which the wind blows, and the Pauls of Tarsus are grateful to island friends for lighting fires to keep them warm during cold rains—these are likewise places of Word-presence, analogies of how God deals with us, of how we choose to accept his Word in regard to where and how we are. Ultimately, we reject or accept that even the rains and the snows are given to us in the warmth and gentleness of God. "Like sun and moon", the Psalmist says of Yahweh, "he will endure, age after age, welcome as rain that falls on the pasture, and showers to thirsty soil" (Ps 72).

There is a sense, I think, in which our spirituality needs regularly this fresh input of nature, of knowing a pasture in the rain, or snow in the mountains that gives waters later in the Summer. We did not create any of this, yet there seems in all of it a word directed to our hearts, probably that of gratefulness is the best, of the fact that something given to us, which we indeed need to exist, is also beautiful and gentle and awesome, like Yahweh.

Christianity is not a "nature" religion, but it is a religion in which nature is a sign, a vestige of the spirit in which we are created. I do not think any spiritual life is complete or even healthy that neglects the pastures and the sands, the thunders and the cyclones, the snows and the rains of this world, made in the Word, which became flesh and noted the lilies and the sparrows, the rocks and the seas, the sunsets and the rains.

26

Wernersville

Situated some eight miles west of Reading on U.S. 40 in Pennsylvania, just after Sinking Springs and just before Robesonia, is the pleasant small town of Wernersville. Perhaps a couple of thousand people live there, in houses of red brick, mostly along the busy highway and a few blocks back. This is the site of the Novitiate of the Maryland Jesuits. I believe Wernersville is the last of the rural, older Jesuit Novitiates still used for its original purpose, institutions in a changing culture perhaps more worth preserving than we might have once admitted. (Wernersville ceased to be a novitiate in 1993.)

At Spring break in 1978, my first year in Washington, during Holy Week, I decided to make the annual retreat, which we Jesuits are happily required to make, in Wernersville, a most hospitable house. Previously, I had made Holy Week stays in such places as Bari and Genoa and Palermo in Italy while I was still there. Wernersville, of course, has nothing like the ancient Catholic spirit of an Italian city. Yet I am inclined to think that such small American towns are very near to the heart of our nation.

The town of Wernersville seemed almost entirely Protestant in religion. Indeed, next to the Jesuit House stood the exquisite Hain's Church of the United Church of Christ, a truly beautiful church whose foundation goes back to 1735. From miles around on my walks, I could usually spot its graceful spire. As is often in Europe, the church is surrounded by a well-kept cemetery, here full of mostly German names. Almost every street in town or road in the countryside bore a name found on a tombstone in this cemetery.

The Jesuit house itself was very well constructed with rather nice cloisters, on spacious ground. Mr. and Mrs. Nicholas Brady, of "Real Lace" fame, gave the building to the Society in 1928. This part of Pennsylvania is most pleasant. I walked most of the country roads around Wernersville—names like Wooltown Road, Gaul Road, Galen Hall, Mountain Home, Showers, Brownsville, Krick. I even took State Hill Road all the way to Reading once.

Spring was not fully revealed while I was there, though several days were mild. Sleet fell on Holy Saturday. Great flights of honking Canadian geese were often overhead, a marvelous sight in their varying V formation. I saw several pheasants, a rabbit, even a raccoon. To be in such quiet country—quiet except for a hazard I shall touch upon in a moment—was a complete change, a touch of the vastness of it all, of the places we do not know about, so we are surprised to find them.

I walked country roads alone, going by many pleasant farmhouses—I recall one with hundreds of chickens, roosters, calves, and pigs. But this reminds me that a sturdy stick is necessary on such a walk. So while I am on the subject of dogs, which is why you need a sturdy stick, I want here to lay down a few simple rules for anyone so bold as to tramp country roads—a joy too nice to miss even with the perils.

(1) Assume that at every farmhouse lurks a dog. (2) Assume further that said dog is meant to protect the turf and all its approaches, including the public road on which you are walking. (3) Recognize that the Law won't protect you. (4) When the inevitable hound comes charging after you—on the average of every fourth house; in the others they are chained, sleeping, or momentarily distracted—face him, stick firmly in hand so he can see it. (5) Expect no help from the owner of the dog, to whom it never occurred that the beast was not harmless to mankind. (6) Do not breathe easier until you are well beyond the farmhouse and said dog has gone back to sleep.

On these walks, I ran into so many dogs of various breeds and shapes that my heart seems still beating faster. Down the road from the Hain's Church, for example, an old farmhouse had two huge German police dogs, chained, but running full blast to break loose so as to get at yours truly as he walked gingerly by. The first two times I went by these snarling beasts, I was lulled into complacency because the monsters were chained. The third time, however, I suddenly realized the larger dog was somehow unchained. I fortunately spotted this before it was too late, quickly took to my heels, and took another road. The dog could have eaten me alive; and, as far as I could tell, this is exactly what he intended to do.

It is the silent dogs that scare one most, though growlers have their awesomeness. Once a big Boxer almost got to my stick before he growled. Another time, near the top of Galen Hall Road, I noticed a woman hanging out laundry, and I foolishly thought I was safe, even though I thought I saw a big black tail in the brush alongside the road. As I got closer, sure enough a huge coal-black Chow or something was on top of me. I froze. My sturdy stick failed me. The end was obviously near. The lady pleasantly yelled at me not to worry. "He won't bite you"—famous last words in my book.

Finally, the black dog slunk back, disproving my thesis that owners never help. The only thing that saved me was the laundry. The lady proceeded to bawl the dog out for going on the road, since its job was only to protect the property. Imagine giving a discourse to a black Chow! Then, feebly, she explained to me that the monster had never seen "a man with an umbrella before".

I was still too frightened to tell her that I was sure that the beast had never seen a man uneaten before, *period*. In sum, you have no rights against dogs, only sticks, luck, and wounds.

Yet the calm rural area of Pennsylvania was worth all the growling, slinking dogs—the hills; the last snow melted while I was there. I saw the first crocuses; I still marvel at the geese in flight. To see many things, I think, you do need at times to be by yourself in some place you do not know.

27

Tommy

My youngest brother's youngest son, Tommy, died on January 30, 1982, in Porterville, California, State Hospital, evidently of some sort of heart problem. Tommy was born with serious congenital disorders and spent almost his whole life as a ward of the State of California. We never expected him to live much beyond infancy, certainly not beyond adolescence. But, with much aid of modern medicine, he fooled us all, somehow. He probably never had a mental development of much beyond six months, but he could crawl about a little.

I remember his smile, not unlike his three older brothers'. He had a definite personality all his own. He was a human being given to us, no doubt, to find out if we were likewise human beings. My brother and sister-in-law in Aptos were always grateful for the quality of care given to Tommy in the hospital, a concrete witness to what ought to be the presupposition of all our laws: that each human life, from its conception, is sacred in all its forms.

Tommy was the fourth son, to be followed by three younger sisters, dear ones, each. He was the only child in the family who was not quite normal. He would have been twenty-two years old on February 13, 1982. You wonder, of course, why God chooses some, not others, especially ourselves. I remember when we realized how serious Tommy's problems were, my brother's saying to me, simply because he was his father, "We will try to do everything we can for him." And they did.

But after a while, I think, everyone began to realize that such a child, who never lived at home, existed for reasons not our own, though he was meant for us too. He did things for you, not you for him. On catching such deformities before birth, many almost automatically recommend, and quite legally, that all such Tommys in the land be destroyed. We saw this trend already during his lifetime. If we should recommend this elimination, of course, we teach something about ourselves, not about what Tommy is. We teach that we claim for ourselves a power not given to us.

When Tommy died, but before I knew of his passing, I was up in New Jersey, where I came across and clipped out an account in the *Trenton Times* (January 30, 1982) of the death in Moscow of Mr. Mikhail Suslov, the chief theoretician of the Soviet Communist Party. Leonid Brezhnev, who was party chairman at the time, flanked by eleven other Politburo leaders at Lenin's Tomb, gave his eulogy:

> While saying good-bye to our Comrade, I would like to tell him, sleep peacefully, our dear friend. You have lived through a big and glorious life. You have done much for the Party and the people and they will preserve the bright memory of you.

Presumably, when Mr. Brezhnev said, "I would like to tell him", he had no thought of life beyond the grave. But as I read that account after I learned of Tommy's death, I wondered what Mr. Brezhnev would have said to my brother and sister-in-law. My nephew lived no big or glorious life; to tell him to "sleep peacefully" seems rather despairing. Nevertheless, it is quite proper in this context to call Tommy's death, as my brother did call it, a "blessing".

Actually, I said to my brother on the phone, rather helplessly, "I will certainly pray for him." My brother replied, "Don't pray for Tommy, pray for us. Tommy has made it. We can better pray to him."

That is, no doubt, the real difference between Christianity and Marxism in the actual context of our lives. Tommy is not just a "memory" to be preserved, though he, like Mr. Suslov, is that too. A life like Tommy's is indeed big and glorious, not so much in our estimate, but before God. As are all children, he was given as a gift, no less than the others, and a suffering too. He challenged our values, our sense of meaning and destiny. If Mr. Brezhnev's eulogy were correct in its implied teaching, we all, as unique beings like Tommy or Mr. Suslov, might just as well despair.

But Tommy was mostly a judgment, not merely on Marxism but also on our culture, which fails to find absolute existence in him, though, thank God, some, like his parents, did. Tommy has a younger relative, now many years younger than he was, a perfectly sound and happy little girl, whom he never could have known. Her mother's doctor advised her father in six or seven ways to abort this little girl. Killer doctors, I call them. Parents have to refuse.

No, the right solution was that sense of personal obligation shown by my brother and his wife, by the State of California, by the little girl's father and mother, in doing what was possible, to tell us that all human life is worthwhile in its particularity, even in our Tommys. We find this out only by first believing it is so.

Otherwise, we are back with Mr. Brezhnev and the abortionist doctor who justify human life in terms of ongoing society, understood on its own terms. We must start at the opposite end, with the life given to us in all its stages, then try to do the best we can for it, as my brother told me so long ago. Tommy's life was worthwhile, and he is with God—both. Anything less, as Mr. Brezhnev's touching but empty words from Lenin's Tomb seemed to me, is despair.

28

In the Shining Light, Destroy Us

For a course I gave in 1986 on political philosophy and natural law, one of the books I had wanted to read, or reread, with my good class was C. S. Lewis' *The Abolition of Man*, a book that I had not taken a look at for some time, though its powerful theme has almost become a part of the way I think. I felt doubly bad about not having read this book more often, since I am constantly referring students to Lewis' remark that someone who has read a great book only once and thinks he is done with it, has not read it at all. Every semester, it seems, I have at least a few students—but only a few, so it is encouraging— who come up to me after reading, say, Aristotle's *Ethics* to tell me gravely it is just another book, as if the problem lies in Aristotle and not in themselves. *The Abolition of Man*, in its own way, I think, is a classic book for our lot.

At the beginning of the second chapter, entitled "The Way", Lewis, without translation—he wrote for literate people—cited the following Greek phrase: *en de phaei kai olesson*. I figured the phrase was from Homer, at the very basis of our civilization, but my dictionary only brought me to brightness of day and destruction. I did not recall the context. Finally, I wrote a note to Father Edward Bodnar, in our Classics Department at Georgetown. He quickly informed me that the phrase was indeed from Homer, from the *Iliad*, where Menelaus is praying to Zeus: "Father Zeus, draw from the mist the sons of the Achaeans, make bright the air, and give back sight to our eyes; *in shining sunlight, destroy us, if to destroy us be your pleasure.*"

When I read this, I smiled again in marvel at the erudition of C. S. Lewis, as well as his sanity. For when I went back to Lewis' context, this particular passage from Homer touched exactly what Lewis had in mind. He had been reading high school textbooks—"the upper forms of school", as the British say. He became increasingly appalled at what he was finding in English literary criticism and writing-books, at the kind of emotional theory erstwhile teachers were putting in the minds of unsuspecting youth. He thought these ideas undermined the very structure of civilized life, because they separated emotional life from the good of *what is*. Lewis wanted us to be sure we knew where these ideas led.

To do this, Lewis pointed out that the traditional ideas of sanity (or natural law), which he held, also could sometimes lead to death. Then he added, "The true doctrine might be a doctrine which, if we accept, we die. [The Aristotelian doctrine that courage is a virtue is an example.] No one who speaks from within the Tao [Lewis' word for natural law] could reject it on that account." [1] Then came, with no further explanation, the Greek phrase: *en de phaei kai olesson*—destroy us in the broad light of day. That is to say, ultimately, we should know why it is we must sometimes do things that may lead us to death, thereby we acquire the emotional support that will enable us to do what is right.

Coincidentally, I had been looking also at Samuel Johnson's *Journey to the Western Isles*. I was interested to see that the famous passage about Inch Kenneth played a basic part in the Lewis thesis: "That man is little to be envied, whose patriotism would not gain force upon the plain of Marathon, or whose piety would not grow warmer among the ruins of Iona." [2] Lewis had just pointed out the consequences of telling the young that when we see something "sublime"—he had

[1] C. S. Lewis, *The Abolition of Man* (New York: Macmillan, 1947), 39.

[2] Samuel Johnson, *Journey to the Western Isles*, ed. Allan Wendt (Boston: Houghton Mifflin, 1965), 111; Lewis, ibid., 18.

referred to Coleridge's waterfall—we are referring to the waterfall itself, and endeavoring to conform our emotions appropriately to something out there, in reality—the lovely waterfall.

But English schoolboys were being taught that when one says the waterfall is "sublime", he is referring only to his thoughts, not to the waterfall. Lewis had great fun with the logic of this curious notion from modern philosophy. Thus, "when I say, 'you are despicable',," Lewis chided, "I really mean I have despicable thoughts." *The Abolition of Man* is a book dedicated to saving the world and our responses to it, to *what it is*, from the destructive logic of philosophies that seek to separate us from what is out there, the sublime waterfall.

The value of Lewis' book, of course, is its capacity to ask about where ideas really lead if they are carried out in the full light of day. They may destroy us without the nobility. The project of substituting the order of being as we discover it for something we make ourselves, so that our emotions are themselves a product of our own fabricating, has totalitarian implications. All of this, Lewis discovered, much to his perplexity, is found in innocuous things like textbooks used in our grammar schools by very earnest teachers. The students assume that they are ordinary language lessons. Lewis talked about "the image of infinite unilinear progression which so haunts our minds". He noted that the nearer we get to the end of the human race, the less the effect our choices or our technology will have, since power depends on posterity.

In this regard, I also came across a little book by Malcolm Muggeridge, called *The End of Christendom*. These were originally Pascal Lectures given at Eastertime at the University of Waterloo, in Canada. After his first lecture, there were a number of questions, one of which was this: "Mr. Muggeridge, what do you have to say to the established Church in the West, which at this point has at least one foot still in Christendom?"

Muggeridge gave this marvelous answer, mindful as it is of

Lewis' logic about where ideas actually might lead us: "It all depends entirely on where you think the other foot is." [3]

If the other foot of contemporary Christendom is, indeed, as it often appears, in the kind of world wherein man creates his own values and future, so that religion functions as a sort of midwife to encourage us to accept this brave new world, then, of course, the self-abolition of man will also entail the abolition of God for the human race. "In shining daylight, we destroy ourselves." This is a prayer no longer addressed by the Achaeans to Zeus but, as C. S. Lewis pointed out, a project of some men to control all the others who still love *what man is*, from nature.

[3] Malcolm Muggeridge, *The End of Christianity* (Grand Rapids: Eerdmans, 1980), 26–27.

29

Being There

As I had not been in San Francisco in the Spring since 1956, I had not realized the beauty of the spectacular display of rhododendrons that appear in Golden Gate Park in late April and early May—a sort of superabundance of beauty, symbolic, I think, of the real mystery of our lot, namely, that we be given so much, not so little. This was 1984, and I walked to the Rhododendron Dell from Irving Street along Ninth Avenue. On the way, I watched an inning or so of a high school baseball game on Graham Field. Then I went over behind the California Academy of Science building to the Dell. In the Dell, there were signs all over, warning: "Don't Pick the Flowers".

Toward me came a young mother giving her nine-year-old son the devil. The boy was sheepishly, yet defiantly, carrying a sprig of just-picked red rhododendron. I was reminded that Saint Augustine's story about stealing the pears for no reason other than because it was forbidden may still be pertinent, even in Golden Gate Park.

I walked out of the Park at Sixth Avenue, over to Cabrillo to return to the University of San Francisco. I crossed Arguello to where Cabrillo makes a jog and becomes McAllister. At the corner of Willard and McAllister, there is a rather steep incline coming down from Fulton Street. I was not paying too much attention to anything, just walking.

On my left, however, coming up Willard toward Fulton was a Pepsi-Cola truck, and on McAllister going about twenty-five miles an hour toward Arguello was a red Volkswagen station wagon. Suddenly, I heard an odd noise coming down the hill. While it happened, I stood there paralyzed in horror.

A young Chinese boy, about fifteen, on a fast skateboard was zipping down Willard just as the Volkswagen went through the intersection. The boy on the skateboard hit the back of the Volkswagen on the other side of the car from my vision, so I did not exactly see what happened. But as he hit the Volkswagen, which had screeched to a stop, I was sure I could see blood and broken life, as the boy seemed to have hit the back of the car head-on.

The terrified young man driving the Volkswagen jumped out and ran to the boy, as did I. Much to our mutual relief, the boy simply got up off the pavement and nonchalantly began to look for the back wheels of his skateboard, which had been knocked off. "Are you all right?" "Yeah, I'm all right."

Well, when we were both sort of relieved that the boy must have managed somehow to stop in time—he was a wiry, agile kid—we both began simultaneously to give him absolute hell for coming so fast on a skateboard into a blind intersection. The driver, in disbelief, asked the boy again if he was all right. The boy, meanwhile, having found the wheels, picked up his skateboard and continued on foot down Willard toward Geary.

The black driver in the Pepsi truck, also in disbelief, shook his head, "You're a lucky boy; you sure you're all right?" All three of us were a bit stunned. How that boy was not killed, I'll never know.

A couple of days later, I decided that I had not walked up to Coit Tower this trip. So I put on some old clothes and wandered haphazardly, finally climbing up the steep hill from the city side. I sat there for a while watching the boats and water, to return to Market Street, where I caught a Number 5 Fulton Street bus. I was rather sore from the walk. I had a seat, but as the bus crossed Fillmore, with another Number 5 bus, mostly empty, immediately behind it, the driver did not stop. Someone yelled out, however, that he wanted off at Fillmore.

So the driver slammed on the brakes abruptly. But when he tried to continue up the hill, the bus stalled and would not move. We all had to get off and onto the other bus. This time, I did not find a seat, but I was holding the bar near the back door. After a block or so, my back hurt, so I gripped the bar on the other side of the bus also. I am not quite sure what I did, but suddenly I was being cussed-out royally, as they say.

I turned around to find an elderly black man berating me with every name in the book. He was evidently slightly tipsy, wore a green baseball cap, weighed maybe 125 pounds, with greying hair. He was quite eloquent in this art, and I was called loudly every "honky" name in the world, some of which not even I had heard of. It reminded me of Professor Henry Veatch's cryptic comment that Jesuits are rather embarrassed to find out that they were innocent of something.

Well, naturally, everyone in the bus was listening to this and looking the other way. I felt isolated. But I figured: ignore it, and it will pass. But the gentleman would not let up. It seems that what bothered him was that I was holding onto the bar of the weaving bus with both hands, whereas in justice I was evidently allowed one only. After another block of this, the Muni driver stopped the bus and came back. He was a burly, black man with braided hair. He went over to the elderly man and simply put his hand on his shoulder and quietly said to him, "It is all right, man, just cool down."

Suddenly, the most astonishing change came over the old man. He became very contrite and said to me, "I'm sorry for using them words, man." Everyone in the bus, especially me, relaxed. The man was quite on stage by this time. He continued, "Why, I should have stayed downtown and gotten good and drunk." Then he looked at me again. "You know", he reflected, "I guess I am just mad at the whole world."

Finally, he announced that he was going to get off at the next stop, Scott or Broderick or thereabouts. Just as the bus stopped, he turned to the folks on the bus, with a worried look, and worried out loud, "Boy, I'm a little afraid to get off this bus and go home, 'cause my old lady is gonna give me a real 'whumpin'." Everyone laughed and wished him much luck.

So I suppose when you go walking in this city, any city, I think, you meet with beauty and near-death, humor and threats, eloquent cussing and calm words. I sort of hoped that the old gentleman's wife did not "whump" him too much when he got home. Too, I hoped the little boy who picked the flowers, contrary to the Park signs, was able to take his spanking.

But I imagine the Chinese boy's mother would never hear of the skateboard and the Volkswagen. We can imagine lots of things about life, but sometimes, being there is beyond anything we might make up.

30

On Elegant Handwriting

On returning to a sultry Washington in 1978, from a summer of ever-refreshing San Francisco, I received, through the chairman of the Government Department, the following notice in my mail box, from the Acquisitions Department at Lauinger Library at Georgetown University. The librarian was returning one of my requests for a new book. The reason for this action was attached:

> Please Print (your requests). Primary word/letter illegible. Is recommender's name Scholl or Schall? Recommendations from Mr. Schall/Scholl have been consistently difficult to decipher. I humbly request you type or print.

Well, this was certainly a confrontation with what was not learned in grammar school!

However, this note did prove, beyond a shadow of a doubt at the time, the superiority of Gleason Library at the University of San Francisco over the library at Georgetown. For at USF, several of my friends on the library staff there claimed to be able at least to read my handwriting. I believe Mrs. Janet Underwood in the Reserve Book Room even claimed the dubious honor of being an expert in deciphering Schall script.

Nevertheless, this communication from the Lauinger Library did give some consolation to my good mother in Santa Clara, California, who for years has waged an incessant, largely unsuccessful campaign to have me type my letters to her rather than write them. Imagine her joy when her son finally acquired a computer!

When I pointed out to her at the time that it is impolite to type personal correspondence, especially to one's own mother, she merely and dryly responded that the purpose of letters is to be read. And, she continued, it is also impolite to expect one to read what cannot be made out. Such clear logic is probably one of the reasons mothers were invented in the first place, I suspect.

Besides my mother, my good friends the Klines in San Jose also greeted the Lauinger Library communiqué with some glee. Jim Kline actually maintained that if he were to take one of my short letters to a drugstore, he could get any prescription he wanted filled. Surely this is an exaggeration, though Kay Kline, his dear wife, claims stoutly that it takes the whole family all evening to unravel what my mail to them actually says.

Indeed, one time when I had been over on Garden Drive in San Jose, where the Klines live, their daughter Collie laughed for five minutes over one of my fluent epistles. But I maintained at the time that seventh-graders should be able to read the English language in whatever form it might appear. Besides, the Klines admitted that my mail is what they called "community-building", as it took all the family members all evening to translate it.

However, let me assure any reader of this discussion on handwriting that I can read my own letters, most of the time. Naturally, since I do not often receive my own letters, this is not much of a problem.

Of course, in my lost youth, I was trained at the Knoxville Grammar School in the Palmer Method by patient teachers. I can still remember laboriously drawing the circles and lines, up and down, round and round. There remain, I know, some sceptics about the efficacy of my efforts, like those on Garden Drive, who have claimed that this was wasted effort. However, I persist even now in thinking that my handwriting is rather elegant, by certain standards, in spite of ample testimony to the contrary from such noted authorities.

Fortunately, my religious training sent me forth from the Novitiate at Los Gatos the year Father James Healy, who has since died, became the Master of Novices. Everyone used to claim he was an expert at telling character from handwriting. But as I am ambidextrous and can write equally well with either hand, I am sure he would never have discovered the real "me", such as it is—unless, of course, the real self is the same from either side.

In any case, I like to write letters. I do not even mind typing them. Typing was the one thing I seemed to have learned in high school in Iowa. Subsequently, it has proved invaluable and the one thing necessary to use the computer, give or take a few minor things. That I did not learn to type perfectly goes without saying. And my friends are silent about whether anything else was learned in those formative years, or since.

They say that handwriting is a lost art. Against much prejudice, I am trying to revive it. So you can never prove by me that it is lost. I do believe, though, that the ballpoint pen proved to be the culprit. My script is fantastic with a goose quill, the kind George Washington used for official constitutional documents. Unfortunately, there are not many geese around Washington, though we do have a few hunters in the community where I live.

But to please my mother, I must still check into a course in elegant handwriting, just to prove a certain hidden talent. I promised the man in the library I would take one.

In the meantime, don't write me. I'll write you.

31

The Man Upstairs

The Greyhound San Francisco Express left from Harrah's Casino in Reno at seven forty-five in the morning. Presumably. Clearly, it is the fastest ground way to return to the City. It was January 2, the day of the Rose and Fiesta Bowls, games I wanted to see. My brother had dropped me off at about seven fifteen. Plenty of time. In the line in front of Harrah's there were only four people.

I figured it was a cinch to get on the seven forty-five bus to return to the University of San Francisco in time to see the games. My considerate brother, who lives in Reno, had asked me if he should wait, just in case the bus did not arrive. It was New Year's and Reno had been jammed. I had taken this bus before so I foresaw no problems. Wrong.

As it seemed to be the height of imprudence to wear a Roman collar to get on a Greyhound in front of Harrah's the day after New Year's, I was in mufti. Seven forty-five, no sign of a bus. About eight thirty, rumor had it that a bus was on its way, but it was a Sacramento local bus. There seemed to be no semblance of lines or order. That always bodes ill.

A very tiny, tough white lady was telling a black gentleman, wearing a gold-leafed New Year's hat from Harrah's the night before, that she was "going to get on this next bus or all of Reno would know about it". She threateningly bared a lighted cigarette. Certainly I wasn't going to challenge her. She had started out behind me in line but had managed to get in front of me.

When the bus arrived, everyone madly jammed in about the door. It was a wild scene. The driver announced that this bus was a local to Sacramento, going to Truckee, Colfax, Roseville, and such places. He maintained that there would be the San Francisco Express in ten minutes. I mistakenly believed him. The lady with the lit cigarette did not, so she went off. I heard no yelps.

Meantime, the folks wanting to go to San Francisco made another queue in the second bus slot. The third slot also was becoming more and more crowded with folks waiting for an Amador Stage going somewhere. The scene was a mess. I lost my fourth-place spot as neither Greyhound nor Harrah's made any attempt to insist on "fair" lines, first come, first served. Clearly, it was instead the law of the jungle. It was every man for himself. I felt the veneer of civilization rapidly shedding off me as I contemplated how to get on the next bus, if there was one. I don't even smoke.

I tried to station myself between both queues so I could make a fast break for whatever lane the bus would come to. About ten o'clock, a bus, this time with a San Francisco marking and mostly filled already, suddenly came around the corner. The driver pulled into the second slot.

I was not in fact strategically placed. Myriads of old ladies, Filipino men, black matrons, and Oriental college students made it look as if I was standing still as they rushed to the bus door. The driver did not even try to get out or propose a fair order. He took about ten passengers, shoved the others out the door, and took off. The pushiest, I noticed, got on.

What to do? I should have called my brother and stayed another day. However, someone asked a harried lady at the bus desk inside when the next bus would be. She said, just to calm things, I am sure, "Twenty minutes". I believed her, as did about ten other folks. This time I was about fifth in line, determined to imitate the little lady with the cigarette.

There was a portly Mexican man wearing a 49ers hat in front of me with a man from Marin County and his wife in Number One position. Two bags without owners were sitting at my feet. Twenty minutes went by. Nothing. Another twenty, still nothing. The little man at the front of the line snapped, "I know they told me a lie inside." The Mexican man reluctantly agreed, as did I.

Some time later, another bus marked San Francisco pulled in. It also was already crowded with pick-ups from other casinos. At this point, two Chinese girls rushed out to claim their bags in front of me in line. This barging-in infuriated a black matron waiting in back of me, with her son who looked like a tackle for the Raiders. She immediately claimed foul of the Chinese girls and, with her son, marched to the head of the line. I was very careful to muscle my way in behind them and the Chinese girls. I was, of course, no longer fifth in line but closer to fifteenth.

The Mexican man meanwhile had gone over to sit down. He had lost out completely. Some very tiny Chinese ladies, now also in front of me, had managed to wedge in six or seven of their relatives. I recalled how the aggressors on the earlier bus had made me, Number Four in line, miss the bus and probably the games. Somehow, I managed, following the Chinese lead, to get on the next bus, maybe second-to-last to get on.

I could see only one seat left, the one just behind the driver, on the aisle. It was full of baggage. I asked the very stout black lady sitting in the window seat if I could sit there. She kindly said yes. Some man in front of me rushed up to put her bags in the overhead racks. I figured she weighed about two fifty. She was wearing a yellow knit pantsuit and had a moustache. I tried to squeeze unassumingly into the too-narrow seat. Close encounters. As the bus pulled out, with me pressed in the front seat, I saw the Mexican man out the front window. He waved good-naturedly as if the world were this way all the time anyhow.

The lady wedged next to me was from the Pacific Northwest. She immediately told me that I was to thank her for getting this bus here to Harrah's in the first place because she had raised hell at a previous casino when the bus did not show up. I thanked her. She next stood up before the other passengers to congratulate the driver. She proposed to take up a collection in his honor. I heard no seconds.

As the trip began, I tried to read the Dante I got for Christmas. The lady—her name seemed to be Miss Emily—began to talk. She told me about everything that had happened to her in her whole life. She was originally from Anacostia, across from Washington. I did not tell her anything. She told me that this bus was going to Portland. I tried to explain, "No, it is going to San Francisco." This was a mistake. "The driver told me this bus was going to Portland." She told me about her job, her family. She had been in Sweden and Germany. "The houses there are like match boxes; they eat good, though."

She told me that her husband was overseas. She lived by herself and had no children. But, she told me, "Everybody loves me. I do good to everyone around me." I figured she probably did in her own way. I sort of liked her, but hoped she would just shut up. In her apartment, she continued, there was no one "except me and the Man upstairs". However, she had photos there of "Martin, the Kennedys, my father", and someone whose name I did not catch. She told me people were amazed to see these photos in her apartment. She thought somebody by the name of "Ragan"—she carefully spelled it out about five times—had paid off millions to Reagan—for what, it was not clear.

She earnestly told me that her father was a good man. She had lots of brothers and sisters and they had a good time. She told me that her father loved three things: "the Messiah, his farm, and his family". She told me also that he weighed 145 pounds. She never once stopped talking all the way to Sacramento, three hours away, except for maybe three minutes when she snoozed near Roseville.

Meanwhile, there was a midwestern farmer in the seat across the aisle. He was telling the driver how corrupt things were in Washington. He also told the driver what a great driver he (the Greyhound man) was. Miss Emily agreed with both of these propositions by shaking her head. She again proposed taking up a collection for the driver. Again no takers.

Every time it looked like I was listening to the Iowa farmer's conversation or watching the snow scenery over Donner Summit, Miss Emily would punch me. I could hear only about every third word she said. She sort of whispered, and the bus was loud. So I pretended to agree with everything she said. She told me that she belonged to some secret organization seeking reparations.

Miss Emily told me that she did not come to America voluntarily, even though she was born in Anacostia. She noticed that both the American Indians and the Japanese had gotten "reparations". Her organization had hired a lawyer for the same purpose, but he was no good. So now they were going after the lawyer who won the Japanese case. She figured to get reparations—$20,000 a person, she calculated—if not exactly from the Man upstairs, at least from the Great White Father with the help of the lawyer for the Rising Sun's Sons.

My neck was getting sore as I listened to Miss Emily. I could not relax because she punched me every time I wandered off mentally. The bus finally arrived in Sacramento. It seemed that Miss Emily had to catch the Portland bus there. She said goodbye and told me to look her up if I ever got to the Northwest. I promised.

Fortunately, no one sat in her seat in the two-hour leg from Sacramento to San Francisco. I took out my breviary and finished my Office. I got back to USF in time to watch the second half of the Notre Dame–West Virginia game and the Orange Bowl. I felt my day complete thanks to the law of the jungle, Miss Emily, Lou Holtz, and the Man upstairs.

32

Bishops and Pale Young Curates

With our mutual friend Terry Hall, I was in Arlington, Virginia, at the home of Michael Jackson—yes, *the* Michael Jackson, of Houston and Cockburn 80 fame. Michael was telling us of the burden of bearing, in his very person, such a familiar name, at the time borne by both a rock star and a local basketball player. But he admitted that one of the high points of his recent life was a conversation with our mutual friend Monsignor Richard Burke at Our Lady of Lourdes Parish. It seems that Monsignor Burke had not been previously aware that there even was a Michael Jackson other than the one who studied Leo Strauss and speculated in vintage wines. In any case, *the* Michael Jackson, neither rock star nor basketball player, who knows my character well enough, deliberately sent me a copy of *The World of Wodehouse Clergy*.[1]

On receipt of this inestimable gift, I knew I was in trouble. Neglecting all else, I feared I would be distracted by laughter, by nostalgia for England, and by the pressing necessity to look up a myriad of new, unfamiliar words like "snaffle" (as in to "snaffle a jam sandwich"), "ferrule", "rubicund", "raredos", "opherys", "zareba", "mangold-worzels", and "stoat".

Obviously, I partially succumbed, and once I was caught in the fight between "Walker", the tomcat owned by the Bishop of Bongo Bongo, and "Percy", owned by Lady Widdrington,

[1] *The World of Wodehouse Clergy* (London: Hutchinson, 1984).

of Bottleby-in-the-Vale, Hants., who had cast her spell over the bishop during a long sea voyage after his retirement from Bongo Bongo, I was a goner. I actually asked Hall and Jackson whether it would have been possible, on evidence of the names of said tomcats, for P. G. Wodehouse to have known the author of *Love in the Ruins* and *Lost in the Cosmos*.

Here, among Wodehouse's clergy—the Mulliners—were wonders beyond my imagination: Gladys Bingley, "a charming girl who looked like a pen wiper"; Brenda Carberry-Pirbright, the daughter of Mr. and Mrs. B. B. Carberry-Pirbright, of 11 Maxton Square, South Kensington; Bernard Worple; the Reverend Trevor "Catsmeat" Entwhistle; General Sir Hector Bloodenough, VC, KCIE, MVO.

Wodehouse's women were invariably stronger than his generally confused men. And Wodehouse had a penchant for the metaphysical—"cats are not dogs", "cats will be cats", and "Muriel Brandsome was incapable of bearing anything in the shape of bossiness from the male".

Wodehouse's stories, of course, assume a married clergy, capable of quoting, in a flash, Proverbs 27:14, Ecclesiastes 10:20, or Esdras 4:41. Once, it seems, the Bishop of Stortford, a man with old-school ties and somewhat trendy theology, was asked to unveil a statue at Harchester, his old school, a statue of an old and rather disliked school chum, Lord Hemel of Hempstead, affectionately referred to as "Fatty" in his school days.

The bishop—one "Boko" Bickerton in his school days—and the headmaster, "Catsmeat" himself, another old boy, having consumed a suspicious tonic called Buck-U-Uppo, invented by a Mulliner uncle, decided to paint at night the new statue of Lord Hemel at Harchester. This they did, only the bishop forgot and left his hat on the head of Lord Hemel. On discovery, suspicion about the culprit was damaging to ecclesiastical decorum.

However, just as the bishop was about to be trapped, a young student at Harchester bravely came forth from nowhere to confess, falsely, that he had done the dastardly deed. The bishop's relief was, to put it mildly, immense enough to make him wonder about his advanced theology.

> The bishop came to himself with a start. He had been think-ing of an article which he had just completed for a leading review on the subject of Miracles, and was regretting that the tone he had taken, though in keeping with the trend of Mod-ern Thought, had been tinged with something approaching skepticism.[2]

The said "Miracle" was caused at the instigation of the bishop's new secretary and curate, the Reverend Augustine Mulliner, who had given two quid to his younger brother, a student at Harchester, for the deed.

When this same Augustine Mulliner decided to marry Jane, daughter of the Reverend Stanley Brandon, he had a difficult time breaking the news to the girl's stern Reverend Father. This was where a little "Buck-U-Uppo" had originally been tested. After a scene in which Augustine had saved the fleeing bishop from a snarling dog, the bishop, on learning of Augus-tine's problem with the vicar, gave him some sound advice.

> "Think well, Mulliner", he said. "Marriage is a serious affair. Do not plunge into it without due reflection. I myself am a husband and, though singularly blessed in the possession of a devoted helpmeet, cannot but feel sometimes that a man is bet-ter off as a bachelor. Women, Mulliner, are odd."[3]

The good bishop's lady, it seems, had insisted on his wearing "woolies" on a warm spring morning, and this had confused him about the distinctions in things.

So the topic of the clergy and their foibles was not unno-ticed by Wodehouse. I am not reading this book rapidly. The very first story began:

> "Remarkable . . . how fashions change, even in clergymen. There are very few pale young curates nowadays."
>
> "True," I agreed, "most of them are beefy young fellows who rowed for their colleges. I don't believe I have ever seen a

[2] Ibid., 28.
[3] Ibid., 15.
[4] Ibid., 7.

pale young curate." [4]

In conclusion, of course, I shall refrain from commenting on these lines, leaving the case to young marrieds like Jackson and Hall. We might conclude with the observation that the "bossiness" of the male and the "oddness" of the woman are mysteries designed to keep us alert to the miracles we are, to keep us, with the clergy, from being too much "tinged with something approaching skepticism", because we can, with Wodehouse, delight so much in the wonderfully curious human condition itself.

33

Empty Churches

The subject of this reflection is not why people do not go to Mass. Nor is it about Protestant churches or Jewish synagogues. Rather, it is about the myriads of chapels and churches that exist in the Catholic world. What are they "for"? Well, no doubt they are places in which the sacraments are enacted, those rites by which we define and practice our relation to God, as the Church teaches. Moreover, they are, often, places of quiet and beauty, of tradition, especially personal memory.

I recall Sacred Heart Church in Pocahontas, Iowa, for example. This is a lovely church, which both of my grandfathers had something to do with building, whose spire can be seen miles down the highway as you come from Fort Dodge through Gilmore City and the East. I remember my Aunt Fran singing beautifully in this church. I remember, as a boy, my grandfather's funeral, and a couple of years later, my mother's. I have this church etched in my memory as a place of worship and prayer. It is just there.

Not too long ago, I was over in Rockville, Maryland. Walking down the road that stretches from the entrance to Georgetown Prep, where I was staying, I came across a local parish church. It was maybe a Thursday morning about ten. I thought I would cross the road and see if it was open—alas, today many churches have to be locked, such is the status of our civility and lack of it. This was the Church of the Holy

Cross. It was open. No one was inside. I went in, sat a while, said a Rosary, and left.

Another day, I was walking along Georgia Avenue and came across another church, St. Catherine Labouré. It was a Friday, maybe three in the afternoon. I went in; a large open church. It was partly filled with the local grammar school children, who were singing the last hymn of the Mass. I sat there awhile. The nun in charge was giving orders about silence, about the fact that the first and second grades were to leave first. The other nuns and teachers were standing by their respective, uniformed classes. The organist was still playing.

I bring this up because I had been reading Edith Stein's *Life in a Jewish Family (1891–1916)*, which had recently been published by the Institute of Carmelite Studies here in Washington. Evidently, after she became a nun, Edith Stein was asked to write her memoirs. She had begun writing of her family and studies while she was still a student of Husserl but did not get back to finishing her account until 1939. She had been recalling her first visit to Heidelberg on her way to Freiburg to discuss her dissertation with Husserl.

This is what she wrote about her visit in 1916:

> But the deepest impressions [of her visit to Heidelberg] were made on me by things other than the Römerweg and the Hirschgraben. We [Edith and Pauline Reinach] stopped in at the cathedral for a few minutes; and, while we looked around in respectful silence, a woman carrying a market basket came in and knelt down in one of the pews to pray briefly. This was something entirely new to me. To the synagogues or to the Protestant churches which I had visited, one went only for services. But here was someone interrupting her everyday shopping errands to come into this church, although no other person was in it, as though she were here for an intimate conversation. I could never forget that.[1]

This was the passage that had struck me so forcefully: that empty churches are not empty, that the custom of dropping in

[1] *Edith Stein, Life in a Jewish Family*, The Collected Works of Edith Stein, vol. 1 (Washington, D.C.: ICS Publications, 1986), 401.

to them to say a prayer, "for an intimate conversation" with God, as Edith Stein observed, is close to the essence of our prayer.

In this context, one other thing has struck me recently. Peter Berger gave the Third Erasmus Lecture at St. Peter's Church in New York. He entitled it "Different Gospels: The Social Source of Apostasy". In the course of the lecture, Berger talked of Saint Paul's bluntly declaring anathema to those who preach a gospel different from his. "Why would Paul utter such an illiberal thing?" Berger tried to speculate.

> I can think of one very good reason indeed [for his doing so]: because *this false teaching denies ministry to those who desperately need it.* Our congregations are full of individuals with a multitude of afflictions and sorrows, very few of which have anything to do with the allegedly great issues of history. These individuals come to receive the consolation and solace of the Gospel, instead of which they get a lot of politics.[2]

It is said that Edith Stein, then a Catholic nun from a Jewish family, was rounded up by the Nazis and sent to the concentration camp the morning after the Dutch bishops publicly protested Nazi atrocities.

Joseph Ratzinger, in his book *Feast of Faith*,[3] remarked that it is those "who think they are too superior to talk simply and concretely of God who are in the habit of talking about 'transcendence' ". I do this myself sometimes so as not, as Strauss says, "to offend the heathen". Sacred Heart Church in Pocahontas, Holy Cross and Catherine Labouré in Rockville, however, stand as silent testimonials of our faith.

The lady in Heidelberg whom Edith Stein saw in 1916 in an empty church, Peter Berger in an analysis in St. Peter's Church in New York City in 1987, and the German cardinal were right. These silent conversations, not with 'transcendence' but with God, about "the multitude of our afflictions

[2] Peter L. Berger, *Different Gospels: The Social Sources of Apostasy* (Rockford, IL: The Rockford Institute, 1987), 14.

[3] Joseph Ratzinger, *Feast of Faith* (San Francisco: Ignatius Press, 1986), 13.

and sorrows", in our churches empty of all but the Sacrament, need to take place no matter what our politics.

If our politics come first, I suspect our churches will forget why they are, most of the time, empty in the first place—that is, to give us room to converse quietly with God. "Pray always", Paul told us. Our pious politics, as Edith Stein quickly learned, will be lethal. What ultimately counts is how we stand before God in those moments when we are alone before him. Empty churches are there for us to exclaim, with Edith Stein, "I shall never forget that", on seeing that just any ordinary woman on her way to shop can converse there with God.

34

Audiences and Congregations

I once attended a lecture at Dumbarton Oaks in Washington, by Paul Hume, the music critic of the *Washington Post*. He observed that audiences at concerts in the Library of Congress applaud each performance three times and three times only. In other words, you can applaud too much.

I went, somewhere about 1981, to hear the excellent Cleveland String Quartet at the Library along with Father Frederick McLeod, at the kind invitation of Michael and Caron Jackson, who had waited in line one chilly Monday morning for tickets. The Quartet received three encores, and only three.

Speight Jenkins of the *New York Post* has remarked on the etiquette and style of audiences. I myself love composers like Rostropovich who will not begin the evening concert until the audience is absolutely silent. Jenkins spoke darkly of wrapper-openers and other chewy types who annoy neighbors at concerts, operas, and sundry performances. In my Roman days, we often used to frequent the Second Balcony of the Opera House, which was usually full of tourists, resident clerics, poorer, often noisy Italians, and other appreciative but impecunious types.

Meekly, for years, I used to sit through it all quietly fuming while someone in the row in back of me whispered out loud in some strange tongue about how they play it better in Dubrovnik. Father Mitchell Dahood, bless him, while he was alive, would tolerate none of this. He would turn around and "shush" the inconsiderate speaker or whisperer or candy-wrapper opener, as the case might be. Elementary justice.

Tickets to operas are not purchased to hear someone from Malmo, Sweden, two rows back, eat bon-bons or hum something off-tune with the tenor on stage doing a far better job of it. Since Father Dahood also looked like Henry Kissinger, then in power, he got immediate results. However, I suspected even at the time that it was difficult for the good people from Dubrovnik or Malmo to believe that Henry K. was ever in the second balcony of the Roman Opera House listening, shushing, to *Tosca*.

Museums are made mostly to be visited by oneself. Concerts need audiences, hearers. (I wonder what my musical sister in Medford, Oregon, thinks of all this theory!) I've often asked myself what is the difference between listening to the same concert on television, or on radio, or on record, and listening in person. The experience is not the same, surely.

Aristotle said that a good appreciator of music should also play an instrument or sing a little, but not too well. He thought that if you play well, you do not have the time for anything else, for the highest things. Somehow, live concerts in empty halls need something more—precisely, audiences.

Too, there are some things for which an audience ought not to applaud. When Luciano Pavarotti did a benefit concert with the Chicago Lyric Opera for the victims of an Italian earthquake, he sang something from Verdi's *Requiem*. I heard it live on radio. He asked the audience *not* to applaud. They didn't, but the fact that he had to ask them not to showed he knew the barbarians were already within the gates.

Sacred music, most proper to churches, should *never* be applauded, in my view, preferably not even in formal concerts (where, unfortunately, too often we must go to listen to it). The current tendency to applaud in churches strikes me as all wrong. There is nothing more powerful than hearing a great work of sacred music to complete silence. Sacred music in its essence is designed to lead us to what is surrounded by but beyond music itself, to what is holy and awesome as such.

Robert Shaw conducted Handel's *Messiah* one night at the Kennedy Center. There was much applause at the end, which, I suppose, is all right. But if the same music were at the National Shrine or the National Cathedral in a specifically religious setting, I should prefer it to be received in silence. I applaud the Emperor Concerto when played well, but I want my Bach mostly in silence.

Today, we speak of our parish as a "congregation", a gathering, with an audience. According to Fowler, the word "audience" originally meant what a king granted to people who wanted to do business with him. It then came to mean a gathering of listeners at a performance. And there are many things which, when heard, we want to "applaud". This word carries the idea of striking something, especially the hand. How astonishing that the reaction of a human being to what is heard as beautiful is to strike one of his hands against the other!

Still, I worry when there are congregations of faithful who applaud at Mass, at a most beautiful Mass. Catholic churches have always claimed to be places wherein the Lord is present literally. The Sacrament was there—"*Tantum Ergo* . . ."

We prayed in churches, where our relation to one another was seen first as a relation to God. This is why we are to be more formal in church. We have a sense of awe that comes when we discover that this world is not enough, that we are each caught up in the presence of the Godhead.

We are all, before God, like Flannery O'Connor before the critic who came up to her and remarked, "That *Wise Blood* was a profound book. You don't look like you wrote it." She answered, "I mushed up my squintiest expression and snarled, 'Well, I did', but at the same time I had to recognize he was right." Perhaps none of us look much like we were made by God, but we were—squinty, snarling, or otherwise. And it is this latter sort of folk who congregate before the altar to listen in silence, even if the singing is lousy. For here is something sacred, a rite, a presence.

The most beautiful sacred music is to be heard in silence, I think. And at times we are to look at our neighbor solely because he was made by God, because we know the reach of our neighbor is God himself, whom, as the First Commandment says, we are to worship above all things.

The clap of the hands is the sign that spirit touches matter when we really know beauty exists outside of us. We know because we have heard it. But in the very clapping, we know there is a beauty that is only hinted at. This further something we await, in silence, I think. For me, Mass ought to be mostly like this—otherwise we will be tempted to lessen what it is we expect. The hearers gather, the listeners see. We do not, indeed, look as though we were made for beauty and divinity. But we were.

35

On the Rights of Women

I once had a little friend (grown now) by the name of Ellen, with whom I managed to go to the movies once in a rare while. It would not be exact to say that I took her to the movies. For actually when you are dealing with films fit for children (on that Saturday afternoon I am thinking about, there were only three movie houses in the city with films proper for children, each of these with a film called *Lt. Robinson Crusoe* as one of the double bill), you do not take them, they take you. For a Saturday afternoon movie is definitely a children's world. It is rather like that sign in the Children's Zoo in Golden Gate Park in San Francisco that proclaims: "No Adults Permitted unless Accompanied by a Child".

Ellen had a little friend, Kelly, staying with her, so we went over to Ocean and Mission, because the girls, when given a choice and without hesitation, wanted to see a sentimental film called *Where the Lilies Bloom*, rather than *Mr. Superinvisible Man*, as the second feature with Robinson. *Where the Lilies Bloom* turned out, surprisingly to me, to be a wonderful movie. So my affection for Ellen, already very high, was even greater when I realized she knew already what this sad, touching movie was going to be about. I probably would have taken her to *Mr. Superinvisible Man*, as it was closer. Droll me.

But here, I want to refer to *Lt. Robinson Crusoe*. It was a Walt Disney "modernization" of the original story, in which an abandoned Japanese submarine from World War II was the wrecked ship, and Robinson's man Friday turned out to be a lovely Polynesian girl whom Robinson promptly named "Wednesday".

It seems that Wednesday's father was a headhunter, no less, with definitely chauvinistic attitudes, which included putting his dear daughter on the desert island because she had refused to marry the man of his choice for her. Naturally, Robinson is quite sympathetic to Wednesday's plight. He is shocked to learn of the backward attitudes of headhunter fathers. He informs Wednesday that in his native country (Lt. Robinson Crusoe was a jet pilot in the U.S. Navy, who was forced to bail out over the South Pacific) "women have rights".

Wednesday was, of course, quite delighted to hear this strange philosophy, but some difficulty with its interpretation seemed likely in trying to prove the point to her chieftain father. The rest of the film dealt with how Robinson set up a loudspeaker, found on the submarine, in the gigantic stone-god called Bauna, whom Wednesday's father consulted for advice.

Bauna, with Robinson's loudspeaker voice, was supposed to inform the headhunter chauvinist that even gods recognize women's rights. Actually, Wednesday ended up falling in love with the innocent Robinson, who had to make a desperate escape from the rejected woman's wrath. The headhunter father naturally roared with laughter at this net effect of "rights".

Kelly, Ellen, and I had to take the Number 14 Muni bus down to 16th Street to transfer to the Number 22 Fillmore bus, to make it back home after the movies. At the transfer stop, in the early Winter evening, many people began to wait about us. A tall, handsome black woman gently sat her little boy, about one year old, down on the sidewalk. He wore big eyes and a lovely red knit suit. He could barely walk. The two girls knelt down and began to talk to him and play with him until the bus came. On the busses, we saw three drunks, some boys whom Kelly suspected of smoking pot or something worse, and crowds of the normal early evening human condition.

I don't think women have rights. That too is probably a mad statement these days. But really, anyone who maintains that women have "rights" narrows them. As we got on the bus at 16th and Mission, there was a tall, dignified black woman of about forty taking care of a wild-looking old man, who was mostly smashed. She let him fumblingly help her on the bus in a way that made it clear that she had to help him. The lady with the little boy, I recalled, had a sad, tired, yet serene look about her. She seemed pleased that the girls had taken care of her boy for a few moments. Ellen and Kelly somehow realized that this was something women do, take care of helpless, or tired, or bombed-out things.

Women don't have rights. They have, rather, graces, and sacrifices, and tolerances, and patiences, and commitments that make the word "rights" sound ridiculous as a term adequate to cover what it is they confront and accomplish in life. I know very few women whom life has treated "justly".

But somehow, I know even fewer women who really expect that it should, and most of these work in universities. Women always manage to find themselves at the heart of those moments in human life when justice and rights seem banal. When someone is born, or someone dies, when someone is sick or stupid or unsuccessful or hurt or hated or disappointed, you usually find women about taking care, doing more than they should, receiving less praise than they deserve. But somehow, they do not much expect that it should be otherwise.

This position is undoubtedly a classic Christian, perhaps romantic, view of things. But I suspect it comes closer to the reality I have seen than any notion that "women have rights". When women start demanding "compensation" in some economic or political sense for all the wounds of mankind that they bind freely, it will be all over. But actually, it will never happen. If you give women a legal right to work eight hours a day, with benefits, at a job of their choice, they will end up working at a second "job" in their family. And the second job will probably be closer to the women's real lives.

It is well and good to talk of women's rights, I suppose, as the Bauna said to the headhunter and his daughter. But it is a funny concept, too, as the native chief saw. Life has something to do with rights and justice, to be sure. We usually assign this area of life to the males, or at least we think we do. It is probably the least important part of life when you examine it.

There are, in my opinion, only two really sensible books on this subject—Chesterton's *What's Wrong with the World* and Gertrude von le Fort's *Eternal Woman*. Perhaps they are not read much, though Ignatius Press has recently republished the Chesterton book. But they fairly well describe the kind of life most women in fact lead and the dignity this gives to them. And that life is not a life accurately described in terms of rights and justice.

Probably the whole essence of Christianity is a commentary on the inadequacy of rights and justice, however unpopular it is to hear this. I have never found it much of a mystery to understand why women are more naturally religious than men. They already know somehow from the time they were little girls like Kelly and Ellen that much more than justice would be expected of them, given to them.

Women have rights? Dear God, that is the last thing life will impose on most of them. The Christian God is said to be a God of mercy. Were he a God of justice and rights, all women would, I suspect, be atheists.

The four orphan children in *Where the Lilies Bloom*, the second movie we saw, buried their father on a North Carolina hilltop in the Great Smokies. It was a tender and moving scene.

"Did you cry when the children buried their father?" I asked Ellen on the Number 14 Muni. "I almost did", she answered quietly.

I sometimes suspect this comes close to defining the real status and destiny of most women—that of "almost crying".

36

On the Pleasure of Meeting in Heaven

On a February evening, I was invited by my colleague Professor Jan Karski to attend a performance of the Washington Dance Society in the Kennedy Center. Professor Karski's wife, Pola Nirenska, was a well-known director of modern dance. The final dance of the evening, set to some music by Ernest Bloch, was entitled "Dirge, 1981", based on the following phrase from the Roman Stoic Seneca: "In memory of those I loved . . . who are no more". The dark mood of the dance did somehow embody the sense of individual disappearance into total oblivion that we often associate with the Stoics, ancient and modern.

I bring up this dance in the light of an amusing incident in the Grand Tour that James Boswell took in 1764. It seems he was in Mannheim on November 7, where he decided to visit the local Jesuit college. Boswell seems to have known of a French Jesuit teaching there by the name of Monier. "He was a black, handsome man, between thirty and forty. He showed me their *refectoire*, but told me that although their college had a good outside, it was but poor within." (What good Jesuit procurator has said *that* before!)

The two walked in the college garden for a while, where they talked of "the favorite subject of the Jesuits, the Catholic controversy". Monier, it turned out, had been in Canada and was thoroughly annoyed at the French for abolishing the Society. "They will see the terrible consequences", Monier warned. "They will see the decline of literature. Not precisely that the Jesuits sustained it all alone, but they aroused emulation." I wonder if we still think this way . . . ?

In any case, Père Monier inquired if Boswell were a Catholic. Boswell replied negatively, adding that "I hope that I shall not be damned for that." He asked Monier, somewhat wickedly, if he thought that he (Boswell) would be so damned. The French Jesuit replied, "Sir, it is hard; but it is absolutely necessary for me to believe it. You have not the excuse of a poor peasant. You are enlightened." To this comment, in a passage I dearly love, Boswell, in the beginnings of the *Aufklärung* itself, added: "I smiled modestly."

Boswell then explained that he was "of no sect", but he believed in Jesus and "endeavored to adore God with fervency". Boswell in fact enjoyed worshiping in the "Romish church", while his own notions of God made him not fear him "as cruel". In reply, the French Jesuit remarked that he was indeed sorry that Boswell was not a Catholic. Boswell, in his turn, noted that the Jesuit was "so agreeable" that he almost regretted that he could not please him. Finally, taking leave in the garden of the Jesuit college in Mannheim, Boswell said to Monier: "Sir, I shall have the pleasure of meeting you in heaven."

How different this was from Seneca and from his friends that "we shall see no more". What is the difference? In his *Notebooks*, Jacques Maritain included a chance correspondence he had with a young man, Pierre Villard, a man of great piety who, in the French army during World War I, was killed in late June, 1918.[1] Villard had lost all of his family and was in search of intellectual and spiritual guidance, which he received from Maritain. This particular correspondence is very moving. Indeed, it may be the most inspiring spiritual discussion of a soldier's relation to God one can find.

Amid the distraction and temptations of combat life, in an attempt to keep a clear conscience and Christian view of life,

---

[1] Jacques Maritain, *Notebooks* (Albany, NY: Magi Books, 1984).

Villard had asked Maritain about introducing seriousness into our lives. "Can total confidence exist if an essential goal is not recognized and practiced?" he asked.

Maritain answered that, of course, we needed a single goal, but that such a goal existed. "It is to do that for which we are made, that is to say, to save our soul, which is not made for the earth or for any terrestrial goal, but to be united with God in eternity. All the rest is purely secondary."

Ignatius of Loyola had said pretty much the same thing: "Man is created to praise God, our Lord, to show him reverence, to serve him, and through these things to save his soul; and the other things on the face of the earth are created because of man, to help him achieve the end for which he was created."

When Villard was killed, Maritain received a letter, June 30, 1918, from Abbé Charles Rolin, "stretcher-bearer Sergeant, 26th Infantry Regiment, 3rd Battalion, Section 126". (The anti-clerical French had drafted priests for regular service during World War I—something, ironically, that did much to reconcile France with the Church.)

Villard "leaves among his comrades and with his leaders many regrets", Rolin wrote, "because for the latter he was the model of a conscientious soldier and for the former of a goodness which touched even the most insensitive." The Abbé then lamented the deaths of so many good young men during World War I (Maritain had already seen his friends Charles Péguy and Ernest Pschiari killed in the war), but added: "Fortunately, thanks to the Communion of Saints, they will continue to live among us, to speak to us, to teach us, to raise us towards Heaven."

Dirges, the excuses of poor peasants, the salvation of the soul, essential goals, deaths at the end of the Great War, the Communion of Saints, gentility in college gardens—let me remind you of these "favorite subjects of Catholic controversy":

65 A.D., *Seneca*, Roman philosopher, suicide under Nero's threats: "In memory of those I loved . . . who are no more".

1541 A.D., *Ignatius of Loyola*, Spanish soldier: "Man is created to praise God, our Lord, to show him reverence, to serve him, and through these things to save his soul . . ."

1918 A.D., *Jacques Maritain* to a French soldier on the Western Front: "Our goal in life is to do that for which we were made, that is, to save our soul".

1764 A.D., *James Boswell* to a French Jesuit in a garden in Mannheim: "Sir, I shall have the pleasure of meeting you in Heaven."

37

Waugh at Christmas

My track record for watching the British TV series *Brideshead Revisited*, when it finally made it to American TV, was one installment seen with my mother in Santa Clara. (In that segment, there was a discussion as to whether actual saints might not prove to be, in practice, pains in certain specific parts of the anatomy.) This loss of *Brideshead* was wonderfully made up by a friend, who sent me the English Penguin edition of *The Letters of Evelyn Waugh*, one of those inestimable gifts which, like *The Letters of Flannery O'Connor*, I shall undoubtedly never fully cease to read and cite.

Several years ago, in this regard, I wrote an obscure essay for *The Way* in London, entitled "Letters and the Spiritual Life".[1] I love letters and have always been struck by their abiding value, from those of Cicero and Saint Paul, to those of Flannery O'Connor and now Waugh. The private letter strikes me as the one form of civilized communication that directs itself precisely to the uniqueness of each person, often better than even conversation does. Letters, like so many of the really good things, can be done again, read and reread.

On December 26, 1932, Waugh wrote to Lady Mary Lyton (whom he affectionately called "Blondy") from this wonderful address: "Hotel Tower, Lots 74 and 75, Main Street, Georgetown". Now, this "Georgetown" was not the Georgetown

[1] This essay is reprinted in my *Distinctiveness of Christianity* (San Francisco: Ignatius Press, 1982), 271–85.

where I normally dwell, but Georgetown, Demerara. Just where this "Demerara" was, I was not quite sure. It could be British Guyana in South America. Yes, I was sure it was. But my dictionary yielded no "Demerara", nor did my coveted *Literary Digest 1929 Atlas of the World and Gazeteer*, something I like to consult now and then, just to find out how the world is not anymore.

Waugh wrote from this Demerara Georgetown:

> So yesterday was Christmas and we had very far-flung stuff—turkey and mince pies and paper hats at Government House and we drank to "Absent Friends" and everyone cried like Mr. Hanson and I thought of you and little Poll and Lady Sibell and Hughie . . . God, how Sad! [2]

On December 23, 1935, Waugh was in Jerusalem, writing to Kathleen Asquith. "I half hate Jerusalem", he lamented. "For me, Christianity begins with the Counter-Reformation and this Orientalism makes me itch." Five days later, however, Waugh changed his "itch" and now loved the place "dearly". "It was decent to have Christmas without Hitleristic adjuncts of Yule logs and reindeer and Santa Claus and conifers." Much of our Christmas symbolism is, we sometimes forget, German in origin, though not "Hitleristic". But we can perhaps forgive Waugh and be impressed by his perceptive worries in 1935.

During World War II, Waugh wrote to Nancy Mitford from a military mission in Dubrovnik in Yugoslavia. "Your letter (written on the 12th) was my only Christmas mail—my only mail for some time—and very nice too." One amusing aspect of Miss Mitford's letter "saddened" Waugh, since she did not say to him thanks "for your beautiful Christmas present of *Brideshead Revisited*. It was a beautiful work". Vanity in hand, he worried, was "it too bad to mention or has V2 [rocket] blown it up?" He teased her, "I know it will shock you in parts on account of its piety." Waugh understood how it scandalized the average garden-intellect to take Christianity

[2] *The Letters of Evelyn Waugh*, ed. Mark Amory (Harmondsworth: Penguin, 1980), 67.

seriously as the grounds for any meaningful drama or view of life. Meantime, while writing this letter, Waugh related that partisans were "celebrating Christmas by firing all their ammunition under my window".

Back at Piers Court in England in 1947, Waugh again wrote dryly to Miss Mitford about his friend John Betjeman, later Poet Laureate of England:

> Betjeman delivered a Christmas message on the wireless. First he said that as a little boy he had been a coward and a liar. Then he said he was sure all his listeners had been the same. Then he said that he had been convinced of the truth of the Incarnation the other day by hearing a choir boy sing "Once in Royal David's City" in King's College Chapel.[3]

Naturally, this was too good for Waugh to resist, so he also wrote a postcard a couple of days later to Betjeman:

> One listener at least deeply resented the insinuation in your Christmas Message that your listeners had all been cowards and liars in childhood. Properly brought up little boys are fantastically chivalrous. Later they deteriorate. How would you have felt if instead of a choir boy at Cambridge you had heard a muezzin in Isfahan?[4]

How wonderful is such chiding—and such logic!

In 1954, Waught wrote to Nancy Mitford from his home: "A happy Christmas, wherever you may be. . . . Children come flooding in by every train. It is rather exhilarating to see their simple excitement and curiosity about every Christmas card. 'Look, Papa, the Hyde Park Hotel has sent a coloured picture of its new cocktail bar!' " This sort of fun is at the heart of Waugh's humor, his wonderful irony and wit, with a touch of sadness and loneliness.

Two years prior to his death (he died on Easter Sunday, 1966), Evelyn Waugh was in Goa, where he returned to his more somber musings. He wrote to his wife and children:

[3] Ibid., 264.
[4] Ibid., 265.

Thank you for your telegram of Christmas greetings which reached me at midday today. . . . Christmas was not very cheerful for me. The Goans keep it strictly as a family feast and strangers are not included in their merry making which consists in exchanging bouquets of paper flowers and eating sweets. I dined and lunched alone at my solitary table here surrounded by Hindus and Jews. The breeze dropped for the day and it was oppressively hot.

Midnight Mass at Old Goa Cathedral was a moving occasion, the great building crowded to suffocation with pilgrims from all over India and Ceylon. No mistletoe or holly or yule logs or Teutonic nonsense. Simple oriental fervour instead. I feel far closer brotherhood with these people than in France or Dursley or Boston.[5]

France I know; Boston I know; Goa I know, but Dursley?

I am glad Waugh wrote such things at Christmastide, that Mark Amory collected them, that someone gave me a present of them. And yet, I still like Yule logs, reindeer, Christmas trees, snow, conifers, mistletoe, holly, and the rest of the "Teutonic nonsense". My last name is not "Schall" for nothing, I guess.

Still, the people of Goa were right about the family nature of Christmas, as were Waugh's own children twitting him about the "coloured pictures of Hyde Park Hotel's new cocktail bar". Chesterton said that at Christmas, we should shut our doors for a time and be with our own, those who begot us, those we have begotten, those who love us and live with us. When we know the Incarnation is indeed the first step to brotherhood, only then can we really talk of brotherhood, be it in Georgetown, Goa, Dubrovnik, Boston, France, Piers Court, Waugh's home, Demerara, or Dursley.

[5] Ibid., 388.

38

A Good Answer

Not too long ago, I received from my friend Terry Hall a sort
of assignment. During Lent, it seems, Terry had been reading
The Private Prayers of Lancelot Andrewes.[1] A certain passage kept
recurring in these prayers which went, in the Morning Prayer:
"A good answer at the dreadful and fearful judgment-seat of
Jesus Christ our Lord, vouchsafe, O Lord." Obviously, certain
kinds of theological persuasion make such a passage meaningless—those that save us all no matter what we do or hold, for
example, or those that think being is nothing, or those that
make all guilt corporate or social.

But Terry Hall is a Christian. He wanted to know something more. As he put it:

> The thing that strikes me about this particular invocation is,
> simply, what can it mean? To put the problem bluntly, I found
> myself asking, 'But what can one possibly say in one's own
> defense on the fearful day of judgment?' All of our sins will be
> laid at our feet, and it will be clear that we are responsible for
> them—so of what could 'a good answer' consist? It is not, I
> take it, as though there will be extenuating circumstances
> which we can claim. So what is the meaning of that phrase?

When I thought about these provocative lines, somewhere in
me I recalled reading something on this topic, something that

[1] *The Devotions of Bishop Andrewes,* trans. John Henry Newman, in *Prayers,
Verses and Devotions* (San Francisco: Ignatius Press, 1989), 155.

had to do with the idea of judgment: that no act is complete until it is finally judged. But I will come back to this.

Terry Hall had mentioned that Walker Percy took the name "Lancelot", for his novel of the same name, from this English divine. Now, it just happened that I had been reading *Conversations with Walker Percy*, a wonderful book, which also had been given to me. I have good students who force me to keep up with them! *Lancelot* received a good deal of attention in these "conversations". And there is a silent priest in the same novel.

Percy reflected:

> At the end of *Lancelot*, I was trying to present two radical points of view, neither of which is accepted by most Americans. One is: Lancelot goes to Virginia for the third revolution, he rejects the world. The other is: Percival [the silent priest] goes to a parish in Alabama, and he hears the confessions of Buick dealers. They couldn't be more different, and yet they have something in common: they both know there is something radically wrong with the world.[2]

Earlier, Percy had remarked that what drives his Lancelot to madness and puritanical revolts (Voegelin's gnosticism here) "is the increasingly bland, permissive Christianity that regards sin as merely a sickness. . . . The book is an attack on the middle ground. It's saying the middle ground is not going to work." [3] That is to say, there is a black and white, a true and a false, while our system is now based on the principle that nothing matters save what we think makes truth. We thus "cheerfully accept the challenge to the womb posed by women's lib" because, for sociological reasons, we think it is a "right" to have dead babies.

In thinking of Lancelot Andrewes himself, I vaguely recalled too that at a bookstore my first year at Georgetown, I had somehow bought, at a greatly reduced price, a splendid book

[2] *Conversations with Walker Percy*, ed. Lewis A. Lawson and Victor A. Kramer (Jackson: University Press of Mississippi, 1985), 211.

[3] Ibid., 155.

called *In God's Name: Examples of Preaching in England from the Act of Supremacy to the Act of Uniformity, 1534–1662*.

I wondered if it contained any Andrewes. Sure enough, it did; three sermons, in fact: "The Meaning of Immanuel: A Sermon Preached before the King's Majestie [James I] at Whitehall on Sunday xxv December A.D. MDCXIV, being Christmas Day"; "A Sermon of Thanksgiving for Deliverance from the Gunpowder Plot, 1605, Preached before His Majestie on the 5th of November 1615"; and the famous "A Cold Coming: A Sermon Preached before the King's Majestie at White-hall, on Monday xxv December A.D. MDCXXII, being Christmas Day".

Indeed, the editor, John Chandos, had a bit of introduction to Andrewes. He lived from 1555 to 1626. He was Bishop of Winchester, a Fellow of Jesus College, Cambridge. He had also been Bishop of Chichester, later of Ely, and participated in the work resulting in the Authorized Version of the Bible. Reading this over, I noticed that Chandos began with a reference to an essay T. S. Eliot wrote on Lancelot Andrewes in 1926. This too made me curious.

I had a couple of books by T. S. Eliot someplace, and after checking my shelves, I managed to locate Eliot's *Selected Essays* and, sure enough, the essay on Andrewes: "Andrewes' emotion is purely contemplative; it is not personal", Eliot wrote. "It is wholly evoked by the object of contemplation, to which it is adequate." [4] This seemed somehow related to Terry Hall's question.

And what about this notion of "a good answer", about which I had been asked? There are two things I further recalled having read of late. The first was an essay of Hans Urs von Balthasar called "The Unity of Our Lives", in his *Convergences*. The second was an essay of C. S. Lewis called "Historicism", which I found in his *Christian Reflections*, and this interested me because I had been reading Leo Strauss' remarks on the same topic.

---

[4] T. S. Eliot, *Selected Essays 1917–1932* (New York: Harcourt, 1932), 298.

Von Balthasar wrote:

> There is someone in whom the elements of our existence, which are cast forth, lost, wasted in the emptiness of time and the impersonal space, are brought together—in their complete deficiency, their powerlessness and their failure. If we are really loved by the eternal Father, then the hairs of our head are numbered by him, our needs are known, our mistakes are regarded with kindness and—through this tireless love which makes up God's essence—compensated for.[5]

"A good answer" at the dreadful Judgment, then, would first of all be a frank recognition of the existence of these acts of ours. I believe the ultimate evil remains not so much in the doing of evil, but in calling evil good. This is what Walker Percy understood to be the real problem with our popular and especially academic religion today.

C. S. Lewis added, "By far the greater part of the teeming reality [of individual human actions] escaped human consciousness almost as soon as it occurred. None of us could at this moment give anything like a full account of his own life for the past twenty-four hours."[6] Yet this full accounting, on von Balthasar's premise, ought to be part of what it is we are, the judgment.

Recently, I had occasion to give a lecture on Aristotle and friendship. A perplexing problem kept recurring. Do we want to know everything about our friends? Do we want to know their faults? Or want them to know ours? In a sense, of course, the answer to this is a hearty "no".

Yet if evil is indeed a lack, as Aquinas held, following Augustine, the reality that is there, the being in which this evil existed, is good. It will remain before "the dreadful and fearful judgment-seat". The only alternative would be for God to reduce us to nothingness. Yet the whole mystery of creation,

[5] Hans Urs von Balthasar, *Convergences*, trans. E. A. Nelson (San Francisco: Ignatius Press, 1983), 124.

[6] C. S. Lewis, "Historicism", in *Christian Reflections* (Grand Rapids: Eerdmans, 1982), 107.

including our own, is continuance in being, even in being that fails. The failures are part of the reality we are. Without them, as it were, we are not we.

Probably the passage in Scripture most pertinent to this reflection is that wherein Jesus began to write on the sand. One by one the accusers went away, presumably because Jesus wrote enough of each one's life for him to recognize himself. "None left?" Jesus inquired. "None, Lord", was the reply.

That, I think, was "a good answer". For it was a judgment of *what is*. There is no middle ground. Judgment is the condition of the everlasting life of each of us.

"I was doing a teary reading of 'The Lord is my Shepherd'," a friend visiting a dying priest friend wrote, "when Father Lietrim died—just stopped breathing. Death is familiar to us all, but somehow it's out of sync—humans should not die. Well, we don't, really, except [that] at some point we are not materially present." My friend herself died a few months after writing this.

That which she wrote, too, is "a good answer", preparing us for that "full account" of the unity of our lives without which what it is we were and are—"humans should not die"—could not continue to be. "What say ye, to drinke *vinegar and gall* ?" Lancelot Andrewes exclaimed before James I on "the meaning of Immanuel" that Christmas Day in 1614. "That is much more (I am sure), yet, that He died: I cannot (here) say *with us*, but *for us*. Even drunke of the cup with the dregs of the wrath of God: which passed not from Him, that it might passe from us, and we not drinke it." [7]

As Lancelot Andrewes put it in the Evening Prayer: "A good and acceptable answer at the dreadful and fearful judgment-seat of Jesus Christ, vouchsafe to us, O Lord."

[7] Lancelot Andrewes, "The Meaning of Immanuel", in *In God's Name*, ed. John Chandos (Indianapolis: Bobbs-Merrill, 1971), 206.

39

On the Lure and Lore of Popcorn

Popcorn, I know, unlike wine, was never mentioned in Scripture. This omission was not, I think, a divine oversight but a reminder that even the faithful might have to await the discovery of the New World to find out all the good things God had in store for them. You will have to remember, no doubt, that these reflections are being written by someone born in Iowa. I still recall that in all the gardens in our neighborhood in my youth, in my uncle-farmers' larger country gardens, there would also be two or three rows of popcorn planted, usually, next to the sweet corn. The sweet corn was for the early Summer. The popcorn was for the Fall and Winter and Spring, and, yes, for the Summertime too. A seed for all seasons, it was.

Popcorn was not exactly something you would kill for, but it certainly was something that you loved to smell and pop. I still cannot pass a place where the smell of freshly-popped corn is coming out and not pause to wonder how one could invite oneself in for a taste. Moreover, I know nothing of the various varieties of popcorn, though I do recall the white and the yellow corn, one having oblong kernels, the other, round. I recall too that not all popping corn tastes the same.

And I fortunately have a friend who, like me, believes that popcorn is not something you remove things from before you eat it. No, sir. Popcorn is not to be stinted nor left to the health-food critics—dare I say "nuts"? If you do not eat popcorn in its natural order, that is, with butter and salt, or in balls of some exquisite sticky stuff, like those my father used to concoct, you are not eating popcorn.

Hence you can imagine how pleased I was to find the entry under "Popcorn" in the *New Columbia Encyclopedia*—the *Britannica*, being British, had very little on popcorn and listed it under "Maize", if you know what I mean. The *Britannica* did say that popcorn was a variety of flint corn, with little starch and no depressions in the kernels. In fact, popcorn is practically devoid of soft starch—which is why I believe certain diets allow it to be eaten straight, in which form, of course, it should never be eaten. It also "explodes" to six or eight times its kernel size because of the moisture in it, hence its name. Popcorn, I insist, requires butter and salt. That is its natural law.

Popcorn was a sort of ceremony in our home in Iowa and remains so in the homes of my brothers and sisters. There were certain rules our dear grandmother, who brought us up, insisted on: (1) If you make it, you clean up the mess. (We sometimes did.) (2) Spread newspapers everywhere so you do not ruin the rugs. (We did, but I noticed that you were likely to find popcorn kernels under the sofas or beds or chairs, in the strangest places, come clean-up time.) (3) Eat what you make. (4) Don't use all the butter. (We did.)

Well, in any case, you probably cannot make enough popcorn, at least the right way, as my friend or brothers make it in the natural order, with butter and salt (and you have to have lots of water too and not intend to eat anything else for at least twelve hours afterward). This is why popcorn is great for evenings in the winter—also it seems to have been created by God to anticipate the long afternoons and evenings of watching football or basketball on TV. If this does not prove Divine Providence, nothing does.

Anyhow, this is what the *New Columbia Encyclopedia* says: "Freshly popped corn seasoned with salt and butter or formed into balls with molasses taffy is especially popular in the United States." I dare say. Well, I hear the Japanese have discovered it for their bars, where it is served like peanuts, at a horrendous price.

And who of us, recalling the amount of popcorn we could buy in our lost youth for ten cents (my brothers and I used to know old farmers in Knoxville from whom we could always get a cheap supply), can tolerate the price of popcorn at today's movie houses, even though we pay it because you cannot go to movies without popcorn. This ten-cent price was during the war, World War II, that is. What we never could really stand was using margarine instead of butter. We still ate it, but it was just not the same. Still, to see how comparatively little popcorn you get these days at the movies for $1.50 almost boggles the mind by comparison.

I know there are today all sorts of popcorn poppers, many prepackaged throw-away contraptions with butter and salt so you never have to do a thing but open the foil. There are big names in the popcorn industry, too, but I don't know any of them. When it comes to popcorn, moreover, the Aristotelian rules of moderation do not apply. If there is not a huge supply upcoming, don't even begin. The stuff is a drug that makes cocaine look harmless. Once you start, you not only cannot stop—if it has butter and salt, of course—you ought not to stop. Good things need sometimes to be savored in their abundance. This is the natural law.

The encyclopedias claim popcorn was found in the graves of pre-Columbian Indians. Bless them.

40

Mexico City

Sometimes, academic enterprises take us to places we would like to see again. Some time ago, on my way back to Rome from San Francisco, while I was teaching a semester in both places each year, I recall having seen in Mexico City some superbowl on a TV station from Brownsville, Texas, while visiting with old friends, Jim and Sheila Freckmann (who since then have been in Yugoslavia, Korea, Vienna, and Athens).

I thought of this superbowl while I was on a second visit to Mexico City, walking through the child-filled Chapultepec Park. I noticed an astonishing number of teenagers and small boys wearing 49er, Pittsburgh, or Dallas Cowboy T-shirts. I saw no Redskins! When the International Studies Association decided to hold their 24th Annual Convention in Mexico City, it was also decided to include a panel on the contribution of religion to politics. As this was a topic I had been thinking about in recent years, I was somehow included.

At that time, in 1983, the peso was about 150 to the dollar, gas prices had just been raised, the weather was perfect. The Mexican newspapers I read were full of rather bitter, ideological, anti-USA editorials. It was like being back in Italy. Gaston Garcia Cantu, for instance, had written in *Excelsior* (April 8):

> In a history like that of the United States, fabricated from immigrants, genocide of indigenous communities, and isolation of nations, it is difficult to establish comparisons to discover

which of its political actions has been more criminal and to infer from it the true spirit of the United States.

Of course, I thought, if such a position were really true, there would be not the slightest difficulty in figuring out the true spirit of the United States, so Cantu was somewhat facetious.

Raphael Oceguera Ramos in the more leftist *El Diario* (April 6) was still attacking Jeane Kirkpatrick's famous essay "Dictatorships and Double Standards".[1] From this essay, Oceguera Ramos derived the very contorted conclusion that she "advocates military intervention whenever it interests the United States".

However, such ideological biases seem both to be a part of the Mexican scene and somehow also of little ultimate importance in such a place. As I wandered through this, perhaps the most populous and highest, large city in the world, I could not keep my mind off of Rome. How many "Roman" things seemed to be in Mexico City. They included not just the Cathedral, which had a John Lateran look about it, but the rhythm of the day—a late dinner, and supper about eight or nine at night.

The very life of the city seemed "Roman", the vistas, the monuments, the water, the traffic, the shops, the newspaper kiosks, the men with straw brooms, the gypsy lady in front of the hotel. I kept asking for things in bad Italian instead of bad Spanish. I went to Mass one night at seven at the Iglesia de la Votiva on the Reforma, near the conference hotel. The church had that warm, open sense of ease with God that I somehow associate with Latin Catholicism.

One morning, as I came out of the Cathedral on the great square in the Zocolo, I walked by the Great Government Palace, down a small side street. People were just setting up their stands, selling every-which-thing, especially newspapers. About fifty yards down the street, I noticed a very old man coming along toward me with a very pretty young girl, maybe six or

[1] This essay is included in James V. Schall, *Liberation Theology* (San Francisco: Ignatius Press, 1982), 162–90.

seven, in a long skirt, probably his granddaughter, walking beside him.

The old man had silver-white hair against his bronzed, handsome face. Over his shoulder he was carrying a suitcase attached to an ordinary rope. About the time they neared me, the old man wanted to switch the heavy suitcase to his other shoulder. The little girl was almost "motherly" toward the old man. As he was struggling to loosen the rope, she got under the suitcase with her shoulder to hold it up so her grandfather could shift the weight. I thought of helping them, but I realized that this is how they got along.

The little girl knew already how to help her grandfather. You could almost see in her eyes that soon she would take care of him. I do not know when I have been so touched by a passing incident. I walked on down the street and went into a chapel, where Mass was going on. I kept thinking that this is really what Christianity is all about, what the little Mexican girl did for her grandfather right in front of me.

Before I had left Georgetown for Mexico City, Father Jim Harley had given me his *Fodor's Guide to Mexico City*. The guidebook listed an inexpensive restaurant called the Circulo Sureste, about a half-hour walk from the conference site. The guidebook also recommended the beer from Merida and the Yucatan specialties served here. Well, since "me and the Yucatan" are not on familiar terms, I thought I would try it out. Something called "Chicken Pebil" was suggested.

The restaurant, when I found it, was very crowded at about two-thirty in the afternoon. Again, I was almost back in Rome. Rushed young waiters found me a table. There were at least three rooms on different levels in the restaurant. I knowingly ordered some soup, a beer, beans, and the said Chicken Pebil. Chicken Pebil turned out to be chicken prepared on a bed of banana leaf. It was quite good, but just the familiar noise and laughter of a Mexican restaurant were worth it all.

Present at the conference were many young Mexican students, who were very nice. But it seemed from their observations that they had simply learned nothing but standard academic leftist revolutionary theory as an explanation of reality, which, alas for them, it isn't. But all of this academic talk seemed esoteric and distant amid the life of such a great city. Life somehow seemed there so much more than the thought. Again I thought of the little girl and her grandfather's suitcase. I was sure redemption still took place out there in the streets before our very eyes, if we would but see.

41

The Real Miracle

Tom and Barbara Donohue—now in San Diego—I had known during my early Roman days, when Tom was in the legal division of the Navy at the U.S. Embassy on the Via Veneto. When I came to Georgetown in the late 70s, they— such was my good fortune—had me look up Don and Connie Kerwin, old friends of the Donohues from New England. So one rainy, wintry night, after getting hopelessly lost and soaked only a few blocks from the Georgetown campus, I finally managed, with help from neighbors, to find the Kerwin home on 45th Street. Don was a pathologist in the G.U. Medical School.

The Kerwins had three young children, the two younger ones adopted. Julie, the youngest, then about six, has always been a special friend. One Spring, with Don's Uncle Lou visiting from Waterbury, and Don's cousin-in-law Ann, we went to Gonzaga High's production of *The Great George M.*, in which Julie, we all thought, was smashing in the chorus.

The Kerwins were a kind of home away from home for me. They included me at Thanksgiving or Easter. I used to wander over for a Monday night football game, when the Redskins were doing something. Don had an extensive beer can collection. Young Don, their son, was a fine distance-runner in high school and later here at Georgetown. I have some photos of us all at a meet in Virginia in the fall of 1978. Connie, in the photo, is serenely watching the goings-on; Julie is clowning with a young friend; big Don is watching the boys at the starting line. The leaves had turned in this scene, beautiful as only northern Virginia can be.

Don and Connie were a particularly well-loved couple. They belonged to the Third Order of St. Francis de Sales and, at one time, to a Jewish–Christian discussion group, and I do not know what else. They belonged to nearby Our Lady of Victory parish, where I recall being present for Julie's First Communion. Don had been on the Admissions Board of the Medical School. He was gentle and good at his profession. He was from Waterbury, Connecticut, and had gone to Fairfield University. His Uncle Lou used to come down on holidays. There would always be a songfest when Lou was about. Lou, as Don happily told me, "did a little vaudeville in his day". Don and Lou could sing almost anything, a real delight once they were warmed up.

Don always limped a bit. He had hemophilia, but we just assumed his medical profession would enable him to cope with it. He never complained, for sure, except for the inconvenience he caused others. Sometime in 1984, Don, then about fifty, developed a rather large tumor in his hip, which pretty much incapacitated him. After a good deal of analysis, he decided to undergo a very chancy, delicate operation at Chapel Hill, in August of that year.

I was in California at the time, but I attended a meeting in Washington in early August, before the operation. When I went over to see him, I rather knew it would be for the last time. A friend of Don's and Connie's, who owned a restaurant on Connecticut Avenue, was over, too. Don was cheerful, funny, as he always was. Nobody knew more about the mechanics of death than Don did, I suppose. He would have been the first to smile at the Gospels' "Doctor, cure thyself" admonition. Several weeks after the operation, Don died and was buried in Connecticut.

Because of a conference I was scheduled to attend, I missed the Memorial Mass here at Dalghren Chapel, where his son, Don, then at Michigan Law School, gave a touching eulogy of his father. However, we had a second Mass at Our Lady of

Victory, where Father Dick McSorley read a brief passage in which young Don said, "When we were praying for some kind of physical miracle for my father, he told me when he was very sick, 'You know, Don, the real miracle of my life is that I have loved and that I have been loved by all of you.'" At the homily in Our Lady of Victory too, some words of Saint Francis de Sales were cited in which Saint Francis recalled that God never takes a harvest unless it is in full season to be taken.

Don Kerwin always seemed to me to be simply a good man—gentlemanly, genuine, humorous, competent, patient, faithful, rather the sort Aristotle referred to when he told us to do in our actions "what the good man would do". As he became more an invalid, Don would read a bit each day from Father Joe Tylenda's new translation of Thomas à Kempis.[1] The difference between the good man of Aristotle and the good man of the Christian revelation probably has to do mostly with the kind of enigmatic suffering a good man unaccountably, by our standards, undergoes.

In the Third Book of *The Imitation of Christ*, Don may have read, "My Son, do not let the work you have undertaken for me wear you down, nor let tribulation dishearten you, but always let my promise strengthen and console you. The reward I offer you is beyond measure and without limit."

We are a generation of Christians who seem to be taught mostly about the world, about "causes", about staying alive, about somebody else's injustices and protests—a kind of horizontal spirituality. This is all right in a way, but the death of a good man, a doctor who knows about death, in what ought to be the prime of his life, of a disease his profession cannot itself handle in his particular case, brings us back to the real miracles of our existence, however long we live, in whatever conditions of gentility or suffering, or both.

The "miracle" of Don Kerwin's existence, beginning with the very fact that he did exist, was what he said it was to his

[1] Thomas à Kempis, *The Imitation of Christ*, trans. Joseph N. Tylenda (Wilmington, DE: Michael Glazier, 1984).

son. Such are, after all, the words we read in the Epistle of Saint John: "We are to love, then, because he loved us first." Such passages of great depth are mostly abstractions to us, I think, until we see them in the lives of friends, who were, indeed, good, faithful men.

42

Spring in Washington

On Tuesday of Holy Week, I was in the old (now gone) Woolworth's on M Street. The day was warm and clear, after three days of windy rain. The very early flowers were out, the crocuses, the yellow forsythia, some white fruit blossoms. A lady ahead of me in line was buying some tennis shoes for one of her children. We chatted a bit. Clearly, she had an accent, which I could not immediately identify.

The lady inquired of me whether the weather was always "like this", a sure sign of a foreigner to these parts. So I asked her if she had just arrived. She was from London, had arrived in New York for the first time the previous day, and was driving with her family to New Orleans. She could not get over how beautiful Washington was. And I thought, "How marvelous to see Washington for the very first time on such an early Spring day!"

And it is so. Washington is a place to which people come in Spring, not for lobbying but merely just to see it. I had walked over to the last half of the Cherry Blossom Parade, about two weeks ahead of the cherry blossoms, but still found a great spectacle of high school bands, with their ever-varying drumbeats and marching gaits.

The first band I saw was from Jencks, Oklahoma; then, one from McKenzie, Tennessee. I recall others from South Jordan, Utah; Perry, Georgia; Strongville, Ohio; and Hoquiam, Washington. The last two were quite snappy bands. It is always a thrill to watch a band stepping with precision and internal discipline down Constitution Avenue, a band with an inner unity, which makes the band live. And I, for one, still love bands that do not disdain to play Sousa marches rather than the latest rock pieces, to which it is impossible actually to march.

I decided to go to the noon Mass at St. Patrick's downtown on Holy Thursday, a church I rather like. As I had not yet eaten breakfast, afterward I walked down Pennsylvania Avenue for a while, via Lafayette Park, and finally over to Reeves Bakery on F Street, one of my very favorite Washington places, a place with real character. I love even the new counter in Reeves. I bought a roll and walked over to the Mall. I sat down on a bench on the inner path, itself angled across from the Smithsonian Castle, to eat the roll. I was doubly hungry because of its aroma and the lateness of the hour.

Joggers passed by constantly. Joggers, I have decided, have changed the face of the land. The Mall from the Capitol to the Lincoln Memorial had always seemed too long, but if you put a few dozen joggers on it constantly, with their strides and togs and huffing, the place is almost intimate. Bemused by the scenes on the Mall, I watched an elderly lady in a red-and-black plaid suit. She was patiently taking a photo of what looked like the ground. Here was one of the most glorious sights in the world and she was taking a photo of dirt! On more careful observation, however, I saw that she was actually shooting, or I should say, snapping a pigeon. This amused me no end. And I suppose pigeons are beautiful in their own way. I can remember doing something similar with the swans along the Thames. In this world, one beauty distracts from another, confirms it, too.

It is good just to take some time off, to walk in a city. You always find parts of it you have never seen before. On Good Friday, I walked over to Catholic University from Georgetown, over 16th Street, cut across Spring Street (was it?) via the Mental Hospital Clinic, to the Washington Hospital complex. On upper 16th Street, I went by the Fourth Church of Christ Scientist, with the announced sermon for Sunday,

"Unreality". I thought to myself, "They are stealing my stuff!" Along the way too, I discovered the statue of James Cardinal Gibbons.

The Good Friday service at the National Shrine was nice. Music there is always in good taste, beautiful. Except for the *Christus*, the Passion according to Saint John was an all-female production. "They are busy observing the letter of the law", I thought, not uncynically. Pilate, Annas, Peter, and Caiaphas were all spoken by female voices. As I left, I ran into my old friend Monsignor John Tracy Ellis. "I see that the Shrine has replaced young men learning how to read the Word of God with middle-aged nuns", I laughed. "Well, you would think that Peter and Pilate should be male voices if you are going to dramatize it", he observed.

I supposed the theological point trying to be made was that even women politicians could be Pilates or Caiaphases, though I have always suspected the Christian tradition did not tend in this direction. The role of women in the actual Passion accounts seems rather different.

On another day, I walked through L'Enfant Plaza at noon. I like the huge fountain there, though the whole complex still seems stark, as if it should be located someplace on the moon. To be human, plazas need people living in them day and night, I think. Further down along the waterfront, the Washington fish market, squeezed away at the far end of the harbor, had more character than the whole area I had just seen. I hope they do not edge the fish market out.

On Holy Saturday, I finally walked from Georgetown to Alexandria along the bicycle path via the airport. This is a spectacular walk on a clear, cool day. The views of the city change the angles of the great buildings, on an arc from the Georgetown Towers, to the National Cathedral, Watergate, the Kennedy Center, the State Department, the Lincoln Memorial, the Old Post Office tower, the Capitol, St. Dominic's slender tower. Sometimes the Capitol Dome and that of the Library of Congress vie for one's attention. The Jefferson Memorial too is always lovely.

This is a city well worth seeing in the Springtime, to behold the sequence of flowers and blossoms, from crocus, forsythia, tulip, various pink blossoms I do not know, cherry blossoms, azalea, and dogwood. I envied the lady from London seeing this all for the first time. But if a thing is worth seeing for the first time, it is worth seeing again and again, I think. One from California, as I am, easily thinks that to see Spring we can dispense with the Winter. But on an early warm Spring day in Washington, with the flowers, one must also wonder about it. Washington has much wrong with it, I suppose, but there is, on a Spring day, something quite right about it, quite worth the trouble to go out and just to behold it.

43

On Fixed Prayer

In her short story "The Deluge at Nordemey", Isak Dinesen told of a certain Cardinal Hamilcar von Sehestedt, who was an anomaly in those Protestant lands of Schleswig-Holstein. "The one remarkable thing about [the Cardinal's] family", we were amusingly told, was that they had stuck, through many trials, to the ancient Roman Catholic faith of the land. They had no mobility of spirit to change what they had once gotten into their heads. "The Cardinal had nine brothers and sisters, none of whom had shown any evidence of a spiritual life." But this is what we wonder about, isn't it—just what are "the evidences of a spiritual life"?

I was thinking of this the other day after I had gone to a parish where, as far as I could tell, the celebrant (not me) made up all three collect prayers of the Mass instead of following the ones in the Missal. At least he did not make up the Canon, though I have seen a bit of this happen, too. I found myself distractedly wondering whether what the celebrant said was accurate, was according to the way the Church prays at Mass? Was what the celebrant made up conformed to any truth other than his own?

One of the signs of a "spiritual life", I think, is the presence of prayers and rituals from childhood, from the generations. I am aware that many today simply have received nothing of prayers from childhood, so they have much to learn on beginning to pray. The father of a friend of mine recently died. On the back of the memorial card of his death was the "Memorare". This was the lovely prayer that my grandmother in Iowa taught my sister, brothers, and me to pray after we finished the Rosary. "Remember, O most gracious Virgin Mary, that never was it known . . ."

Spontaneous prayer, to be sure, has become a sort of "in" thing. And, as the *Spiritual Exercises* of Saint Ignatius, among others like the pentecostal groups, have taught us, this is a good thing in its proper place. Nevertheless, our prayers should conform to what is specifically taught in the Church, which herself has often spent centuries the better to clarify them for us. Our prayer ought to conform to the truths of faith.

Something may be said also for the fifty different versions of the "Our Father" in English or French. But somehow it seems that at our most profound moments, it is not only comforting but necessary that we pray, old and young and in-between, pray aloud with the very same words. Nothing is more touching for a priest, I suppose, than to listen to one of his little grandnieces or a child of one of his friends recite for the first time, in company, haltingly, "In the Name of the Father, and of the Son, and of the Holy Spirit".

"The advantage of a fixed form of service", C. S. Lewis wrote to a lady on April 1, 1952,

> is that we know what is coming. *Ex tempore* public prayer has this difficulty: we don't know whether we can mentally join in until we've heard it—it might be phony or heretical. We are therefore called upon to carry on a critical and devotional activity at the same moment: two things hardly compatible.
>
> In a fixed form, we ought to have "gone through the motions" before in our private prayer; the rigid form really sets our devotion free. I also find the more rigid it is, the easier it is to keep one's thoughts from straying. Also it prevents getting too completely eaten up by whatever happens to be the preoccupation of the moment (i.e., war, an election, or whatnot). The permanent shape of Christianity shows through. I don't see how the *ex tempore* method can help becoming provincial,

and I think it has a great tendency to direct attention to the minister rather than to God.[1]

I have always had a real concern about this latter notion of a clergyman or minister deflecting prayer to himself. So have the classical spiritual writers. Nothing should frighten a priest more than the thought that people are coming to Mass or Services simply because *he* is saying it or preaching at it. Christianity, of course, is a religion that speaks through men, but it has always suspected that holiness and eloquence, or grace and personality, are not simply co-terminous.

Neither eloquence nor a pleasing personality ought to be downplayed. They too are gifts, but what is said or repeated ought not to be things that a talented Christian clergyman or layman simply makes up and "shares"—awful word—with whoever happens to be standing by. The *ex tempore*, valuable as it can be, in my experience is almost always more narrow and less freeing than the precise, "rigid", accurate forms of prayer that embody the simplicity, eloquence, and authority of the ages of the Church.

Our prayers and creeds and formulae of address to the Lord God should be, in large part then, classical things, prayers and teachings everyone has memorized and repeated with long habit. We should recite and sing creeds and Rosaries and teach our children from the very beginning to do so. We should be able to recite the "Our Father", the "Hail Mary", the "Memorare", the Acts of Faith and Contrition, and the Apostles' Creed even before we know about what they mean, so that when we finally do understand what they mean, we will know them, and how to say them familiarly.

On February 16, 1826, Eckermann spoke with Goethe about a "curious" poem of his that had appeared in Frankfurt in 1776. Eckermann remarked, "It is without doubt the oldest of all the known poems of Goethe. Its subject was Christ's descent into Hell, and I found it striking that the religious way

---

[1] *An Anthology of C. S. Lewis: A Mind Awake*, ed. Clyde S. Kilby (Harvest Book, New York: Harcourt, 1968), 147.

of seeing things had been so familiar to the young scholar." But when we think of this, what is more natural than to suppose that Goethe had learned the creeds by heart in his early German youth?

Something may be said, no doubt, for finger painting in catechism class or Sunday school, in order to find out what "original" thing the little tykes might have dreamed up. But I suspect what will serve a child or adolescent more in the long run are those age-old prayers, devotions, and creeds that have come to us from earliest times and that teach us the "permanent shape of Christianity" before we even realized it had a shape. It is to these prayers that we and others can return when we want to pray together in those ultimate moments in our public and private lives, in this world wherein life and death and destiny confront us where we uniquely are.

44

The Sons of the Pioneers

My Uncle Tom Hart's last farm in northwest Iowa was a few miles from a town called Pioneer. Even by Iowa standards, Pioneer was a very tiny town. Compared with it, Gilmore City, where my uncle did his trading, was a flourishing city and Pocahontas, the county seat ten miles down the highway, a veritable metropolis. Pocahontas had maybe 2,000 citizens, not a few my relatives. But Pioneer, as I recall it now, on a hot Summer afternoon, was a place with several large grain elevators, a railhead, dusty roads, a few houses, and a saloon, where you could buy some groceries also.

The very word "pioneer" is, of course, one of those essential ones we need in order to discuss and describe America. We all are offspring of "pioneers", even the Indians. We are a people who do a thing first, when it is still risky and unusual. In a way, the unknown is part of our national heritage. The Oakland Museum—that marvelous California place—once had a display about early flying in the San Francisco Bay area. It included some movie photos based on Professor Montgomery's famous first plane at the University of Santa Clara.

The videotape on this flight recalled for me some of the atmosphere and astonishment in a small town some sixty or seventy years ago when a plane first landed in a nearby field. The movie footage showed the stunts and the bravery of the local gentry who were foolish enough to pay to go up "in one of those damn contraptions".

The word "pioneer" seems mainly to be associated with taming new lands or disciplines, but it has gradually come to be applied to new risk or achievement in any field. We have "pioneers" in aviation, music, art, sports, even government and religion. So, I suppose we are all "sons of the pioneers" in a way.

One of the peer-group pressures we grew up with in the small Iowa high school I attended was that we were not supposed to like the prevailing Country and Western music that ordinary folks seemed to like. Actually, I rather liked this music, but I never told anybody until it became somewhat of a fad to like "Bluegrass" in Washington. Country and Western music, I know, is not Beethoven or Bach, though, like theirs, it is often very religious. Yet I have never believed that simply because something was not as good as the best, it therefore was bad. Fortunately, there are tremendous variations of the good. One of the great mysteries of creation is precisely this variety in what is in fact good.

Even at that distant time, I remember hearing the Sons of the Pioneers, and over the years their "Cool Water", "Back in the Saddle Again", and "Tumblin' Tumbleweeds" were frequently played on the radio. I always would listen when I heard them sing. In any case, I could not imagine this organization—with the almost prophetic name—was still about. So one Summer when I noticed they were performing at the Boarding House on Bush Street in San Francisco, I had to see them.

Their show was simply perfect in its own kind, basically straight, smooth Western music, some clowning, yodels, a sense of sentiment about our most typical music. The present five Sons are second-generation Pioneers. The last of the original group has since died. Yet the Sons of the Pioneers seem to go on forever; I think, and Plato implies, that in fact all music does. Their music is infectious. They wear ten-gallon hats and white Western suits, carry a steel guitar, and sing in perfect harmony—all of which blends together to create something unique. With their music, there is a thoroughly happy evening, something you could feel that everyone there also sensed.

Something as nostalgic as "The Red River Valley" is always

welcome in a world that is like this famous valley, from which "they say you are going". Country, Bluegrass, and Western music is unabashedly patriotic and religious. It sings of betrayal and loyalty, of workin' on the railroad and cheatin' hearts. On Country and Western radio stations today, what is usually heard is that music recently manufactured in Nashville. Much of it is not bad. Some is very good. I once had a chance to be present at a recording session in Nashville. So I have a certain sympathy and admiration for this particular creative process that produces new Country music.

Yet the Sons of the Pioneers, I think, represent an older tradition of Western music, a kind I just like, a kind that is difficult to come by any more unless you happen to notice that these Sons of the Pioneers are still singing in an improbably named establishment called the Boarding House in an unlikely San Francisco. Somehow, you think they should be in Oakland, or San Leandro, or even in Cow Town in San Jose.

But one thing I like about San Francisco is that its worldly sophistication is catholic enough to include something old and perfect in its own kind. Joel Slevin wrote in the *San Francisco Chronicle* of the performance I attended: "The only way the show could be improved is for Boarding House owner David Allen to push all his tables and chairs in a circle, and build a campfire in the middle of the showroom floor."

The evening I was there, no campfires were a-glowing on Bush Street. The audience was just too absorbed in the kind of music the Sons of the Pioneers remembered for us all there, the kind of music that perhaps best reveals our risky American origins and equally risky future. A couple of days later on Public Television, I heard "The Songs of World War I". These songs and those of the Sons of the Pioneers reminded me again of that notion of Plato's, that if you want to know what a people is, listen to what they sing and what they listen to.

The fact that the Sons of the Pioneers are still around singing about their "Cool Water" is among the most refreshing things about our culture, a reminder of what was, of *what is*, of what has not yet come to us.

45

"Ubi Amor, Ibi Oculus"

The German philosopher Josef Pieper is a favorite of mine. I want to talk about his book *Only the Lover Sings: Art and Contemplation*.[1] The lovely title of this wonderful little book is taken from Saint Augustine: *Cantare Amantis Est*. The eight brief essays in this small book are on leisure, music, contemplation, and sculpture. They are touching continuations of Pieper's moving volumes *Leisure: The Basis of Sculpture* and *In Tune with the World: A Theory of Festivity*. We find here also familiar thoughts from *Josef Pieper: An Anthology*, one of the most insightful books I know.[2] I have always loved *In Tune with the World* with a particular enthusiasm, while *Leisure* is Pieper's most influential opusculum.

Pieper begins *Only the Lover Sings* with a discussion of the difference between work and leisure. In reading Pieper, it is difficult not to wonder about the relation of Pieper's warnings on the dangers of "work" mentalities in modern philosophy to the Holy Father's almost rhapsodical praise of work. No doubt these contrasting approaches can be reconciled, though I have never seen this done in any formal fashion. John Paul II is concerned with redeeming work so as to show that even in his

[1] Josef Pieper, *Only the Lover Sings: Art and Contemplation*, trans. Lothar Kauth (San Francisco: Ignatius Press, 1990).

[2] Josef Pieper, *Leisure: The Basis of Culture* (New York: Mentor, 1963); *In Tune with the World: A Theory of Festivity* (Chicago: Franciscan Herald Press, 1973); *Josef Pieper: An Anthology* (San Francisco: Ignatius Press, 1989).

pedestrian deeds in this world man has a deep dignity. *Laborare est orare.*

On the other hand, Pieper is very much attuned to the destruction of the contemplative and its replacement by the mentality of modernity that allows nothing to exist but that which is the product of man's work. Work of its nature has the characteristic of being for something else, even if it is worthwhile doing. Pieper is concerned to defend the fact that there is something that is "for itself", something intrinsically worth doing.

Pieper's concern is about these things that are worthy in themselves. Our response to *what is* is not itself in the nature of work, but in the nature of praise and festivity. "We work so that we have leisure"—Pieper cites this famous phrase from Aristotle. The root of the highest things is ultimately indicated by the only response we can give to the *what is* we do not make—praise. The arts have their roots in this response to what is given to us, what originates in what we did not cause ourselves, even when, as in art, we do originate something.

Pieper's second essay is entitled "Learning to See Again". This is not an essay in ophthalmology, of course. Pieper thinks our ability to "see" is declining, even should we have twenty-twenty vision. We are so inundated by sights that we see nothing. "To *see* things is the first step toward that primordial and basic mental grasping of reality, which constitutes the essence of man as a spiritual being." This reflection leads Pieper to speak of the importance of sculpture. "Nobody has to observe and study the visible human face more than the one who sets out to sculpt it in a tangible medium."

These reflections on sculpture and music are surprisingly incarnational. Indeed, what is even more surprising is Pieper's reminder that the Greek and Latin words for the highest activity—theory and contemplation—themselves mean to behold, to see—not to think.

I have often been struck by the kind and amount of attention that Plato and Aristotle paid to music in their writings on ethics and politics. Pieper's explanation of the reason for this concern is most welcome. Music is not indifferent to the fate of any republic, any less than painting is, or sculpture. "Music prompts the philosopher's continued interest because it is *by its nature so close to the fundamentals of human existence*." These fundamentals are not primarily words.

Music responds to the search for the good that constitutes our lives in their living. To see music as entertainment alone is to miss its depth, its potential both for good and for evil. Music can order our souls to evil if we but let it, which is one reason why Plato and Aristotle were so concerned with it. "What does matter, however, is to recognize at all (*and* to put in the right order!) the intimate relationship between the music made and listened to in a society on the one hand, and the inner existential conditions of such a society on the other—no different than in Plato's time!" We will not order our societies if we do not first order our souls. Such observations were made by Josef Pieper during the intermission of a Bach concert in Essen in 1952.

Pieper's three lectures on sculpture have a particular loveliness. In Greek mythology, the Muses were called into being because Zeus, after ordering the world from chaos, asked the other gods whether anything was missing. After thinking about it, they decided that what was missing was someone to affirm what had been created, someone to sing the praises of what existed. The Muses exist first to remember what exists, then to sing of its wonders.

Many things that exist, however, are in danger of being forgotten. The first Muse is memory. Both priest and artist, Pieper thought, are connected here. "Here we somehow sense the artist's inner relationship to the priest, who is called, above all, to keep alive the remembrance of a face that our intuition just barely perceives behind all immediate and tangible reality—the face of the God-man, bearing the marks of a shameful execution." At Mass, after the Consecration, we specifically "remember" these things, for they define what we are. The artist can be at home in the Cathedral when he sees the marked Face.

In a passage mindful of the *Phaedrus* and *Symposium* of Plato, dialogues that Pieper loves, he wrote of the work of his friend, the sculptress Hilde Schurk-Frisch: "To see in contemplation . . . is not limited only to the tangible surface of reality; it certainly perceives more than mere appearances. Art flowing from contemplation does not so much attempt to copy reality as rather to capture the *archetypes* of all that is. Such art does not want to depict what everybody already sees but to make visible what not everybody sees." Some things we do not see if we do not remember, if we do not gaze, if we do not listen. But things not seen *are*, as Saint Paul said.

Pieper loves the ancient phrase from the mystics, *Ubi amor, ibi oculus*—where love is, there is our eye. He is at pains to show the relation between our contemplation and our incarnate reality. Some things are seen only if we love them, perhaps even our faces. This applies first to one another, first to God. "I hold that this is the specific mark of seeing things in contemplation: it is motivated by loving acceptance, by an affectionate affirmation." Ultimate joy, Pieper said in his *Anthology*, is to be able to say, "It is good that you exist". Like the ancient Muses, we affirm that *what is* is good, even when its existence has nothing to do with us.

In a remarkably beautiful conclusion, Pieper links the Platonic concept of beauty to mystical contemplation and to the fact that we are ultimately seeking God in all our loves and all our contemplations. Pieper notes the German expression "*sich nicht satt sehen können*", which means that there are things we "cannot get enough of". Pieper says that this is the ultimate meaning of contemplation and the arts. They enable us to remember and praise what exists as a gift, for its own sake—what we did not make but what exists.

The first meaning of what we "cannot get enough of" can be seen by an example. The example Pieper uses is simply that "new parents 'can't see enough' of their baby". But this sort of experience of "not getting enough of" makes us realize that there are experiences that simply must remain unfulfilled, even in their fullness.

Those . . . who have—perhaps painfully—experienced and accepted, even in the delight of their beholding eyes, that ultimately their longing will not and cannot be fulfilled, those will be unable to create mere pleasing, agreeable, frictionless art. Konrad Weiss once remarked, "Contemplation will not be satisfied until blinded by the object of its ultimate desires." Such a statement almost leads us beyond the confines of this world.

Of course, that is precisely where it does lead us. Josef Pieper knows this and wants us to know it, too.

Laborare est orare. Ubi amor, ibi oculus. Cantare amantis est.

As I hinted in *Another Sort of Learning*, we need not despair about education in the highest things so long as Josef Pieper is about to address such words to our souls.[3]

To begin his book, Pieper presented two brief classical citations. The first, as I mentioned, was the title, from Saint Augustine: "Only the Lover Sings". The second is from Joseph de Maistre, who knew his Augustine. It reads: "Reason speaks in words alone, but love has a song". Both Plato and Saint Paul would be pleased with such thoughts.

[3] James V. Schall, *Another Sort of Learning* (San Francisco: Ignatius Press, 1988).

46

Speechless in the Presence of God

In the Responsory for the Office of the Third Friday of Advent, we read: "For if one hopes, even though his tongue is still, he is still singing always in his heart. But the man who has no hope, no matter what clamors and shouts he makes to be heard by men, is speechless in the presence of God." The virtue of hope requires that there be an object of hope, supplied by faith; otherwise we are locked into ourselves. The distance between singing in our hearts and empty, clamorous shouts is indeed infinite.

This responsory was based on the Discourse on Psalm 37 by Saint Augustine, whose whole life was an effort to articulate what was in his restless soul. Augustine observed poignantly:

> There is a hidden anguish which is inaudible to men. Yet when a man's heart is so taken up with some particular concern that the hurt inside finds vocal expression, one looks for the reason. And one will say to oneself: perhaps this is what causes his anguish, or perhaps such and such has happened to him. But who can be certain of the cause except God, who hears and sees his anguish?

We are almost incapable of imagining that our real anguish is not heard by someone. Indeed, Saint Thomas in a way posited this realization as one of the needs we have for revelation itself: our incapacity to believe that our inner thoughts do not have a listener. On the other hand, if we lack hope, we exclude even this possibility, not from God's side but from ours.

Not too long ago, I was at a noon Mass in a university town in Virginia. It was in fact the Feast of the Immaculate Conception. In his homily the priest explained, referring to the Confiteor at the beginning of Mass and relating it to the feast, that we should be sorry for our "sinfulness". I said to a friend later that this seemed wrong. We do not confess our "sinfulness" but our sins.

If we think that what we actually confess is our state, original sin, then implicitly we make some sort of divine claim to redeem ourselves when we think our confession makes a difference. We acknowledge our sinfulness, our condition, no doubt, as an intellectual proposition, as a truth of the faith. But we do not substitute this doctrine for the confession of our sins as such, as if somehow our existence in the world were merely some sort of theological problem.

Boswell tells us that in 1779 he was not at all diligent in keeping his journals of Samuel Johnson. All that he had were scattered notes. Among these he found the following passage for Wednesday, March 31:

> When I [Boswell] visited him [Johnson] I confessed an excess of which I had very seldom been guilty; that I had spent a whole night in playing at cards, and that I could not look back on it with satisfaction; instead of a harsh animadversion, he mildly said, "Alas, Sir, on how few things can we look back with satisfaction."

Presumably the "excessive" playing of cards might have something to do with original sin.

But as to confessing the situation to Johnson, what was important was Boswell's own sense of disorder. Johnson's response was one of strict orthodoxy. We look back with little satisfaction on things we actually did, not on abstract truths or theoretical propositions. This realization need not deprive us of "singing in our hearts" when we hope, however, because hope not only includes the fact that sins can be forgiven but acknowledges that our "condition" will continue as long as we do hope.

Perhaps Jimmy Durante had it right. In his book *Good Night, Mrs. Calabash*, William Cahn recounted this incident:

> In 1938 when Jimmy heard of a campaign to clean up his beloved Broadway, he protested: "Whata dey wanna go messin' around for? Whatta dey wanna scrape up da choon gum offa da sidewalks for? Maybe dey wanna have a Park Avenoo over here instead of Broadway?
>
> "Leave it alone or it won't be Broadway no more . . . Don't put no constrictions on da people . . ."

The other side of all this sinfulness-condition is that it is the condition we are in. If we put too many constrictions on the people, they will not be people. The effort to impose some sort of perfect order on us because few of us are satisfied with our actions is the real temptation. The "choon gum" will, alas, remain on lots of "da sidewalks". The Christian answer is, and always remains, not to remove sinfulness by ourselves but to forgive sin in the name of Christ.

Saint Augustine was right: "There is a hidden anguish which is inaudible to men." We will be "speechless in the presence of God" if we do not hope in him. We are to be forgiven our sins even in our sinfulness. "Alas, Sir, on how few things we can look back with satisfaction." "But who can be certain of the cause except God, who hears and sees our anguish?" "For if one hopes, even though his tongue is still, he is still singing always in his heart." Between the playing cards and the "choon gum" there remains hope, provided we don't want to move Park Avenue over to Broadway or confuse our sinfulness with our sins.

47

On Practicing What We Preach

Walking slowly down M Street in Georgetown in mid-November, in the latter stages of my gout, even while the Catholic bishops were meeting at the Hilton, I noticed an odd headline in a *USA Today* automatic kiosk. It blared, "Church Says We Must Practice What It Preaches". I checked this wording at the next kiosk too, but I did not buy the paper, unfortunately. So maybe the headline read, "We Should Practice What We Preach", or even "The Church Should Practice What It Preaches", but I doubt it.

Anyhow, I got to thinking about this headline as I continued down toward Connecticut Avenue. I wondered what it meant. For example, we hope the Church does not mean that everyone should practice what he (just anyone) preaches. That would make, say, Hitler a great Christian, because he did just that, practiced what he preached. In my oddly titled *The Praise of 'Sons of Bitches'* I wrote an essay to the effect that "sincerity" was "the most dangerous virtue" for this very reason.[1]

I was reminded of this topic when one of my former students gave me a book titled *The Theology of Peanuts*, which showed in one series Linus and Charlie Brown looking over a stone fence. Linus mused, "When I get big, I'd like to be a prophet." As they walked on, Charlie explained, "That's a fine ambition, the world could always use a few good prophets."

[1] James V. Schall, *The Praise of 'Sons of Bitches': On the Worship of God by Fallen Men* (Slough, England: St. Paul Publications, 1978), 53–62.

But suddenly, he turned to Linus seriously, "But the only trouble is that most of them turn out to be false prophets." As they went on in single file, Linus concluded, hopefully, "Maybe, I could be a *sincere* false prophet." I would add only that these latter, sincere false prophets are the most dangerous kind.

Furthermore, I trust it is still—one must be cautious—theologically untenable to hold that everyone can, unaided, practice exactly what the Church teaches. Grace and mercy, words rarely heard in these days of justice and self-actualization, are still needed. Officially, at least, we are not Pelagians who work out our own salvation by our own theories for our own final goals, with little fear and no trembling, except for perhaps The Bomb.

On the other hand, if in fact everyone suddenly began to practice what the Church taught, it would cause economic and political chaos. Jails would empty. Brothels and abortion mills would close. Defense plants would shut down. No one would need much insurance. The home safety and protection industry would go bankrupt. We would not need to fear pickpockets, footpads, felons, drunken drivers, embezzlers, or opium peddlers. Sam Spade, Lord Peter Wimsey, Father Brown, and Ralph McInerny's detectives would be rendered unintelligible to the next generation, as in fact would the whole human condition.

When clerics and other pious folks (not necessarily the same, to be sure) begin to tell us that we should actually practice our faith, they usually imply, not overly delicately, that we don't. And that, presumably, is why the world is so badly off, even when we have a pretty respectable income and education. Likewise, there is a whole industry of ex-Christians and non-Christians who take great comfort in pointing out the considerable distance between announced moral criteria and actual performance among Christians, or anyone else, for that matter. "Hypocrisy" is indeed a favorite, though feeble, excuse many give for not believing. Yet hypocrisy attests to a standard.

Chesterton, in a famous passage—I do not think he wrote any other kind—remarked that the Christian faith has not been tried and found wanting, but rather tried and found difficult. We are cautious of those whose beliefs always rule their practices. This is why we have the word "fanatical" and the word derived from it, "fan", to suggest a rather profound difference of spirit in relation to one's ideas or loyalties.

Yet if we suppose that the reason everyone is *not* a believer is because some individual believers are rotters, we soon arrive at some very untenable positions. The New Testament recounts several instances wherein our Lord does a remarkable good deed, only to have those who observe it immediately go out and plot his death because he did something good.

Indeed, several passages in the New Testament seem to suggest that "the good" will be rejected *because* it is good, especially in the "latter days". This is merely another way of recalling that men are constituted with a radical freedom that enables them to reject *any* preaching or example, enables them to call what is evil good and what is good evil, then proceed to follow their "calling" fanatically. We are not to be coerced into Paradise.

Consequently, when the Church tells us to practice what we preach, we must hope its preachers still recognize that the world is full of finite men, that the doctrine of the Fall is not so demythologized in practice that the lot of most normal folks can no longer be comprehended by these same preachers. The tares and the wheat, I believe, intermingle until the end, even, most obviously, in ourselves.

But when the Church teaches us to practice what we preach, we also hope its new-found "compassion" is not so self-righteous that it excludes the poor and the weak from their own moral dignity on the grounds of some neo-Rousseauist theory about sinful structures or social sin, which insists on locating evil outside of most human hearts. We are very near to reducing most people to "objects" of "concern"—or, to put it differently, we are very near to handing over the essential decisions about moral worth to the manipulation of the ideological state or collectivity.

To practice what we preach, then, can also mean to impose a supposedly pure ideology on the people for their own "good", however well it might or might not fit them. Such social theory also enables us to locate the origins of evil not in the human mind and heart, but in classes and groups, in abstractions. We should note with considerable attention that *all* totalitarians practice exactly what they preach, insofar as reality permits them to do so.

So let those who preach to us at least be those who still know about the Fall, who understand why men can fail, who see the human dangers in "demanding" that we practice what we preach, lest we lapse into ideology in the name of religion (alas, a well-trodden path). We ought to be virtuously virtuous, as Aristotle remarked, that is, freely so. Meanwhile, Aquinas observed that we should not expect everything from the law. If this sounds like a plea for the imperfect, the hypocrites, and the rotters against the revolution of the saints, so be it. What is different today is that the ideologies are preaching perfection, while the clerics are seemingly extolling politics. No one seems left to preach to us poor sinners.

48

On Fishing

The "Bay-to-Breakers" foot race in San Francisco was something I figured that I should not miss—watching it, that is. So I walked down to the Four Mile marker just inside Golden Gate Park, off the Stanyan Street corner on Kennedy Drive. The leading runners came by me about five minutes after I arrived there at 8:15 A.M. or so. They were so far ahead of the massed pack—some 70,000, they say—that to call it a "race" was an exaggeration.

But, never having witnessed the darn thing, I was not prepared for the effect of the thousands of oddly shaped and garbed folks who eventually passed by me, running, trudging, jogging, crawling, limping, or otherwise ambling along. Evidently, they were enjoying themselves immensely. But I did not weaken. I did not decide to run next year. So relax there in Kenya, Ibrahin Hussain, who came to be the winner in San Francisco!

They call this race from the Bay to Ocean Beach an annual "event", and so it is. A nice lady standing next to me told me that she had let her husband off at the beginning and she would join him when he reached the four-mile mark. He finally showed up, not exactly last, but about number 45,984 or so. I knew two priests from the University of San Francisco community were out there giving their all, but they never surfaced in the mass of humanity. A nun I knew, however, trotted by to say, "Hello", and in a very creditable position, not far from the front of the women runners.

Another evening, a Wednesday, when admission was free, I went over after supper to see the Grant Wood exhibit at the De Young Museum in Golden Gate Park. Actually, after talking to a friend about it, I had gone over on Tuesday afternoon, only to find it closed. What! Aren't museums supposed to be open all the time? But somehow the normal $2 fee at a museum changes its character for the average man.

You no longer, as in the old days, just "drop in" to see something special or at random. You feel, when you pay, that you have to see everything. Painting especially, I think, needs not to be rushed, needs not to be seen in crowds. "Don't you pay for everything else?" someone logically asked me, on hearing my theory. Someone has to pay for it, I guess, and paying taxes for it is perhaps the world's most expensive way to pay for anything. But still, the human spirit is a delicate thing.

I once (May 1984) did an article in *Crisis* entitled "War and Poverty". It began with the following sentence: "Glancing through some current newspapers stacked haphazardly on a grand piano where I am currently living in San Francisco . . ." About a month later, I received an unexpected letter from Professor Edward Capestany at the University of Scranton, whom I had met about a year before when I was there for a lecture. Bemused, he wrote a brief, sympathetic parody on the particular sentence, a sentence worthy of the *New Yorker*'s end-of-the-column files. Professor Capestany wondered how life in San Francisco was actually going, what with Schall living there on that grand piano!

I mentioned this inquiry to Father C. M. Buckley— obviously a mistake. I had excused myself by saying I had evidently placed my modifiers in the wrong place. He dryly commented that this was but one of my problems, putting my modifiers in the wrong places.

Later this same week, my brother, then in Aptos, and his neighbor, Jerry Harris, bit the bullet and took me fishing with them in the Sacramento River Delta, up along Frank's Tract. It was a spectacular day. We got up at 5 A.M., had a trucker's breakfast at Brentwood, rented a boat, found a store to sell me a fishing license ($17 a crack now!) and bait, and headed up the channel from Sandpiper Slough. One forgets how many inland waterways there are in the Delta above the Bay Area. My other brother used to have a boat up at Pittsburgh, so we had been in the area before. We got the boat at a place called Sam's Boat House. The boat had a six-horsepower Johnson outboard motor that never missed a beat.

Sam told us where to fish. We had brought a map of the area, on the back of which it said that for the best fishing spots, always ask the people who rent boats. So we did. It was pretty windy. We tied up to some rushes and got no bites all morning, though the view of Mt. Diablo was very lovely. We were fishing with sardines. Finally, for lunch, we found a place called Carol's. There, my brother, who was beginning to think he should have gone to the horse races at Golden Gate Fields, found out about a place where at least catfish were said to be biting. No striped bass were being caught yet. So Jerry Harris piloted us to the spot, which, according to the map, had deep water.

Sure enough, I caught a rather nice catfish, though Jerry Harris had previously got one only as far as the boat. My brother, also a Jerry, who does not hold my fishing abilities (to mention no others) in the highest esteem, was rather astonished at my performance with his good fishing pole. I believe I caught another one before the two Jerrys began to get some visible action. We caught about a dozen catfish and headed back, immediately taking a wrong turn to go half an hour the wrong way in the Delta maze. We finally got back to Sam's Boat House, rather, I believe, to the surprise of Sam. We cleaned the catfish—something I used to do as a boy in Iowa, but that I had to relearn. We drove home by a beautiful back road (Walnut–Vargas?) through Livermore.

When I go fishing, I often recall the passage in the Gospels about fishing. The Apostles themselves, except for Matthew, I believe, were fishermen, told to become "fishers of men". What does this mean? A friend of mine in St. Louis used to call fishing "basically boring", which I suppose it usually is. Yet if we assume that we never quite know just when, whether, or what will strike our lines, fishing seems exciting. Fishing seems the most apt description of how the Lord works with us. I guess he figured that most men and women for most of mankind's history would know enough about fishing to get the point. And it is also some comfort, somehow, to know that the Son of God knew about fishing. I wonder if they had catfish in the Sea of Galilee?

Meantime, we froze the catfish, not without calculating that, with license and all, they were probably more expensive than any fish course available on Fisherman's Wharf. We are told to "fish or cut bait", "never give a sucker an even break", "cast our nets on the other side of the boat". Well, on a day on the Delta, you begin to learn something about such language, and why the Lord might have chosen fishermen to spread his Word when he dwelt amongst us.

49

On My One-Eyedness

Milton, I recall, wrote a poem on his blindness. This chapter will not be so poignant or so profound, but it will deal with seeing and not seeing with our very eyes. The difference between being blind and having one eye, as I have recently learned, is in a way infinite. If you have one eye that functions well, you see. You are not half-blind even though you do not see with the range that you do with two eyes.

At the end of July 1989, I was strolling across the Bridge on M Street as it goes out of Georgetown. I noticed some sort of blotch in my left eye. Even I knew it was not normal. After supper that night (it was a Saturday) I was sitting on our roof-garden overlooking the Potomac, and I noticed that everything had become cloudy and obscure. I talked to a friend of mine, a good nurse. She told me to get to the emergency room of the hospital as quickly as possible.

I did this. I got there about eight o'clock. They had to find the two young women doctors on call; one was swimming but rushed right over. By midnight, I had been diagnosed with a torn retina and some bleeding. The next morning, I was given a laser treatment. A couple of days later, I was at lunch down on 18th Street when I noticed that I could not see a darn thing out of the same left eye. So back I go to the doctor. He tells me that the eye is very full of blood. Evidently a vessel had again broken. He decided to wait to see if the thing would clear by itself.

So we waited a couple of months, but nothing cleared. This doctor then recommended a vitrectomy, a sort of pumping-out of the fluid in the eye in which the blood was blocked. Once into this operation, it was discovered that the blood cells in the meantime had formed a membrane on the retina. Some of these clottings were cut off.

However, about a week later, it appeared that the retina was detaching. This required an emergency operation on a Saturday morning. The eye was given a buckle to hold the retina. But neither of these operations seemed to do what was anticipated—during the process I learned a lot about the prayer "Lord, that I may see". My local doctors seemed to be at a loss as to what to do. I suggested we should go elsewhere, maybe John Hopkins or the Wills Eye Clinic in Philadelphia.

Thus, on a Thursday, I found myself facing a third operation in about three weeks. Again I had to arrange for my classes to be taken care of; I really learned to appreciate generous colleagues and friends during this period. I had to call my family in California and to prepare my soul for yet another bout. The operation was at St. Joseph's Hospital in Baltimore, where there is a retina center.

The new doctor seemed to be really a wise, practical man, that kind of common sense that knows about particular problems and difficulties such as I was having. The new doctor did not say much. I asked him what my chances of seeing were with yet another operation. He sort of grunted and told me that he didn't give percentages. He said that if he did not think he could help, he would not do anything. This was fine with me, the sort of good sense that I needed.

So the third operation. The retina was again re-attached, some blood removed, things adjusted. Would I see again? Well, maybe something. The lens was removed on the third operation—that meant a contact lens eventually, once the eye settled down. After the third operation, I saw very little, some shapes. This was what I could expect. The eye is a tough organ, I was told, but you have to let it heal.

After another ten days, the third operation failed. The doctor tried a fourth. The same result. Again everyone pitched in. Just before Christmas, when I had planned to visit the family in California, I went in for a check-up. I was put into the hospital for the fifth time. It was the longest night of the year, December 21. I was not allowed to eat or drink all day. The operation did not occur till six in the evening. I could not have been more uncomfortable. You hurt after each of these operations, but also just with the tubes and needles.

After the fifth operation, I was very punchy. (I know—most people could not tell the difference.) I woke up at some awful hour. I was thirsty, miserable. About seven in the morning, I was taken to the doctor's office. I could tell something was wrong. A somber doctor barely looked at the eye. He told me grimly that the fifth operation was a failure. He put in a wider buckle. After two and a half hours, the eye began to fill up again. That was it: I would not see out of that eye again.

That evening, a former student and her cousin from England came in to visit me. I would be taken back to Georgetown the next day. I was sober. I gathered my things. It was by then December 23. I had obviously long since dropped plans to spend Christmas with my family. However, my friends Denise and Dennis Bartlett and their boys, who had taken care of me after the previous operations, took care of me that Christmas. My face was swollen. I had a big patch on the eye. I knew I would have to live with one eye. Yet, somehow, the Bartletts and their friends made it a happy Christmas for me. I talked to my family in California. It was all right.

Now, I know that listening to or reading about other folks' operations is not always the most exciting of topics. My eye is mine, so naturally I would like it to see what it can. The other eye since then has functioned effectively. I have been getting about with one eye since July. You can do it. Lots of folks have one eye and get along fine. I know that now.

After the first operation, I managed to go back to class for a day before they bombed me with the second operation (for which I had about two hours to prepare). I told the class of the situation—before the operation you could not tell there was anything wrong with the occluded eye. After class, one young man came up and put his arm around my shoulder and told me, "It's OK, Father. I have had one eye all my life. You'll be fine." I was pretty struck by that remark, I must say. I have a nephew with one eye, aunts with detached retinas, so I am aware of this situation.

A couple of days after the third operation, I was still in the hospital in Baltimore. I was on a floor with the eye patients, but also a varied assortment of illnesses were in rooms on that floor. I really was in no mood to wander about. Nurses in a hospital attend to you when you need something—water, eye drops, pressure taking. The last nurse I had there was very good. The old gentlemen with whom I shared the room was just awaiting tests, so he was a bit worried. The nurse said to me, "Oh, Father, you are the least sick on this floor, so I get to you last." Naturally, I thought I was practically dying; my head hurt; I was uncomfortable. But I knew she was right.

I said to a friend, "I learned from this experience that I am not a good 'sufferer'." She laughed and assured me no one was. That was the whole point of pain and suffering. On the other hand, I remembered what I had been going over with my class from Aristotle: the notion that pain or fear is something given to us, over which we have some control, more or less; that we should learn to rule it, somehow.

And I remembered that I am a Christian. You are given suffering for others too. You realized all sorts of people prayed for you. I had asked my class to pray for me before I went to the hospital the second time. One girl wrote a note to tell me she had said a Buddhist prayer for me. We too often forget all those for whom we ought to pray. If there is suffering along the way, that too is to be incorporated into our prayer.

In the meantime, I realized that I will never see anything with the left eye again. It had been a good eye for almost sixty-two years. I saw many wonderful things with it. I know that. The last time I had been in a hospital—except for a brief bout in a hospital in Santa Monica in the 1950s—was when I was about five or six, to have my doctor-uncle remove my tonsils. I figure, on the whole, I have been pretty fortunate. I was the least sick on the floor, and having one eye is a blessing.

But what to do with the non-seeing eye? One doctor thinks the left eye should be removed, at least for cosmetic reasons, to be replaced with a glass eye. So far the unseeing eye does not give me much trouble. When the pressure in the eye is down, however, as is the case with a detached retina, the eyelid droops because the curvature of the eye is not correct. This causes me to look as though I am perpetually winking—not a good idea in my profession. Many folks suggested I wear a patch, like a Hathaway Man or Moyse Dyan. I bought one in Pasadena and tried it out for a couple of days. As I still need my glasses for the good eye, the patch made the glasses sit wrongly on the bridge of the nose. I suppose I could have adjusted to that, but the patch was uncomfortable.

The solution to this by-no-means-ultimate problem I owe to my younger brother, Jerry. He enters a yearly horse-racing handicap tournament at Cal-Neva in Reno, where my other brother, Jack, used to live. This is a kind of annual event where we go to cheer Jerry on. He needs it. A fine example of brotherly love.

I happened to be in Reno for this occasion some months after the final results of the operations. One afternoon, I was in the betting room with Jerry. He went over to make a bet. He came back to say, "Come with me, I think I have the solution to the eye problem." We walked over to the betting area. "Take a look at that big man with the cigar", he told me. Across the room was a man puffing on his cigar and watching the latest race on the screen. He had on a regular pair of glasses in which one lens was darkened.

This seemed the ideal solution. It told anyone without his asking that something was wrong with one eye. But the arrangement was also convenient, part of the glasses you wear anyhow. No patch or glass eye to bother about. So when we went back to Santa Cruz, the local lens dealer made one lens in my glasses dark, and I have been satisfied with the solution ever since. Folks are used to me, and I am used to the reality of one-eyedness.

It says somewhere in Scripture, "If thine eye be lightsome, thy whole body will be lightsome." It is true. Our eyes, like our other senses, are given to us that we might perceive what is not ourselves. If your eye is working well, you do not even notice it. If you notice your eye is an organ of sight, it is because something is in it that should not be there.

Why do we see at all, even with our one eye? It is, I think, so that our whole body be lightsome.

50

On Sitting Down and Waiting

Sometime in October 1936, Ronald Knox gave a sermon on Saint Mary Magdalen, the traditional model of the contemplative life. He observed:

> The world . . . does not understand the love that waits, any more than the love that weeps. It is so impressed with the feeling that this and that needs doing here and now that it cannot wait for God's signal; cannot realize that He has His own way and His own time for doing things, and, in consequence, a great deal of activity is wasted in overlapping, and misdirected effort, and fussiness.

"Fussiness", it seems, consists in doing what is not yet to be done, or in overdoing what we will do anyhow. The notion that God's ways are not ours is a difficult one. Whatever can be said for a theory of human action consequent on grace (we are not Pelagians), the fact remains that we want "our" form of salvation, our form of action to substitute for God's peculiar ways. This human form is usually the modernizing social-activist heresy, so prevalent among us, absorbing our energies into ideologies and calling this virtue.

Years ago, in Naples, I think, I came across a citation from the medieval English mystic Richard Rolle (d. 1349) on praying while sitting down. We used to be taught, it seems to me in early religious life, that sitting down was the least propitious position for praying. Kneeling was the thing. But what with

Russian and Oriental bowings or lotus positions, and Muslim prostrating, kneeling is out. In fact, in so many of the chapels I know, the kneelers have been removed mostly by fiat, together with statues and a multiplicity of candles. No helps but pure mind. We are used to Saint Paul's idea of "praying always", to be sure, and we can no doubt "pray in action", as Saint Ignatius of Loyola used to say, presumably even while we are jogging about or closing a big deal at the Chicago Board of Trade.

However, I chanced to come across an essay on Richard Rolle in a *Downside Review* (April 1983), one of the few Catholic journals that has managed to keep its lively sense of tradition. Sure enough, there was the citation about praying sitting down—though in Latin, not the stately old English translation I recalled from Naples. My version will have to do here:

> Thus, as I looked over Scripture, I found and knew indeed that the highest love of Christ consists in three things: in fervor, in song, and in sweetness. And these three, which I experienced, are not able to persist without great quiet. And so if I wished by standing or walking to contemplate, or even by lying down, I saw that many things would be deficient for me, and I felt myself almost desolate. Hence, by this necessity, in order that I might both have and persevere in the highest sweetness, I elected to sit down.

Now, I suppose that any discussion of the best physical position for praying—kneeling, standing, sitting, walking, or lying down—will seem rather "fussy" when the main question is whether we should pray at all.

In this connection, in her *Interior Castle*, Saint Teresa of Avila was certainly to the point when she said, "I do not call that prayer in which we do not consider with whom we are speaking, nor what we are praying for, nor who we are who pray, and to whom; and though prayer may be sometimes without these considerations, they must have preceded it." So our very capacity to pray is, in the Christian view, itself a gift. It is a gift to pray—a properly human activity, which will normally include some attention to what goes on in our mind and likewise what goes on in our bodies.

I like what C. S. Lewis said in this connection:

> There is no good in trying to be more spiritual than God. God never meant man to be a purely spiritual creature. That is why he uses material things like bread and wine to put the new life into us. We may think this rather crude and unspiritual. God does not. He invented eating. He likes matter. He invented it.[1]

This means, I suppose, that God has his own ways for creatures for whom matter is normal, for whom sitting in great quiet will not likely be an easy or common thing, however much we ought to take a stab at it.

Yet we humans, in our very selves, are the location where matter and spirit are fused so totally that we are simply "one person" for whom both matter and spirit are everyday parts of our realities. Prayer naturally will include kneeling, or sitting, or standing, or walking, whatever suits us, without simply ignoring the positive effort we must take to do as Saint Teresa taught us—the to whom, by whom, for what we pray.

Saint Ignatius, in teaching us how to say the Lord's Prayer, observed:

> that the person, kneeling or seated, according to the greater disposition in which he finds himself and as more devotion accompanies him, keeping the eyes closed or fixed on one place, without going wandering with them, says, "Father", and is on the consideration of this word as long as he finds meanings, comparisons, relish, and consolation in considerations pertaining to such a word.

Even in the spiritual life there is probably a case to be made at times for letting our eyes wander about God's lovely creations, as Ignatius himself did in his famous "Contemplation for Obtaining Love".

We should not, either, forget what Ronald Knox said of Mary Magdalen, that our weeping and our waiting, even what

[1] C. S. Lewis, *Mere Christianity* (London: Fontana, 1961), 62.

we waste, are not designed to substitute for God's graces and ways, but to respond to them. For this latter, I think Richard Rolle had his point—we do need times of great quietness and for sitting down, to listen, to recognize that the whole universe is not composed of ourselves alone. Yet the universe does contain us, each of us, in a plan we did not make, but are given.

When we know this, we can, perhaps, act in a world of matter that God likes, which he is redeeming, but not in a way we would have thought up ourselves, if it were up to us. When the Apostles were told to sit and watch in the Garden while our redemption was being worked out before their very eyes, most of them went to sleep. I have always been glad that our Lord's rebuke of these Apostles was so mild. He really does like matter and those composed of it, spirit and all, sleepers and sitters though they be, too fussy usually to comprehend fully the wonders they have been given.

51

On Its Being Already
Tomorrow in Australia

Easter is the central mystery and feast of the Christian faith. Likewise, it is the only promise to mankind that ultimately means anything. The greatest, perhaps only service the Church can perform for each of us is to be sure that we hear this message, this doctrine, as it is, not as some theologian, or preacher, or philosopher might mitigate or lessen it in his speculations.

Aristotle, in his discussion of friendship—a discussion to which the doctrine of the resurrection is ultimately related—remarked that no one would want to receive all the blessings and goods of the world on the condition of his becoming someone else, not himself. That is to say, the doctrine of the resurrection of the body is unbelievable mostly because it does promise final beatitude not to the vague world of "humanity" down the ages, but to each of us, in our particularity. To teach anything less is to teach despair—something, alas, not infrequently taught in higher academic circles, for credit yet.

What I especially like about the orthodox Christian doctrine is that I did not make it up myself. In fact, it is the last sort of thing I would have ever concocted on my own. That is, what is presented, defined, in the tradition on this topic is much more glorious, more romantic even, than any more sober liberal view that would supposedly give us everything but what we might actually want. "Nothing is more repulsive to me than the idea of myself setting up a little universe of my own choosing and propounding a little immoralistic universe", Flannery O'Connor wrote on St. Patrick's Day, 1956.[1]

A friend of mine wrote to me of a priest friend of hers, who learned he had serious cancer. "Poor man," she reflected in the most basic of terms the laity teach the clergy, "his voice was cracking as he told me of his troubles. Such a cruel time for us poor humans, when we each must directly face the fact of not existing in the only manner we have yet experienced." This is the orthodox Christian terminology, even when, like my friend, we now exist in the manner we have not yet experienced.

In a *Peanuts* episode, Marcie and Peppermint Patty have just listened to a campfire speaker talk about the world's last day. This speech frightened Patty, so she could not sleep. "What if the world comes to an end tonight, Marcie?" Marcie replied, with clear logic, "I promise there'll be a tomorrow, Sir . . . In fact, it's already tomorrow in Australia." But Patty is still worried: "He said we're in the last days, Marcie." But Marcie just turned over and said, reassuringly, "Go to sleep, Sir . . . The sun is shining in Australia."

This conversation is just wacky enough to be wonderful. Don't worry about the end of the world, because, at the end of the world, in Australia, it is already tomorrow.

Samuel Johnson was accustomed to take Easter as a serious occasion for self-reflection and prayer. He was quite conscious of how little, often, we improve, even when we try. In 1765, he wrote in his Easter meditations:

> I propose again to partake of the blessed sacrament; yet when I consider how vainly I have hitherto resolved at this annual commemoration of my Saviour's death, to regulate my life by his laws, I am almost afraid to renew my resolutions.

Yet Johnson, of all people, would have understood about the sun shining in Australia and the folly of our immoralistic messages to ourselves that would leave us content with our own

---

[1] Flannery O'Connor, *The Habit of Being* (New York: Vintage, 1978), 147.

world. The real despair is to believe that there is nothing to renew, that we are as we are because we are already as we ought to be. My friend was right: we do not yet exist in the manner which we have not yet experienced, in the manner promised to us.

The *Chesterton Review*, that inexhaustible source of sanity, redid an essay of Chesterton on birthdays, in which he pointed out the central and basic nature for us, not of the things we make but of the things we are given. The most difficult and wondrous things, I have always felt, are not what we "make" but what is given to us. I do not say that to knock what we make; quite the opposite. But the fact is that all the highest things—truth, wonder, friendship, joy—are, in the final analysis, simply given, almost as if such things already exist in some personal way, and we are merely in a kind of vale of shadows waiting for them to break into our world, like the light in Australia on the last day.

Chesterton wrote on the first day of Spring, 1933:

> Modern thinkers of this kind have simply no philosophy or poetry or possible attitude at all, towards the things which they receive from the real world that exists already; from the past; from the parent; from the patriotic tradition or the moral philosophy of mankind. They only talk about making things, as if they could make themselves as well as everything else. They are always talking about making a religion; and cannot get into their heads the very notion of receiving a revelation. They are always talking about making a creed; without seeing that it involves making a cosmos. . . . There is a whole problem of the human mind, which is necessarily concerned with the things it did not make; with the things it could not make, including itself. And I say it is a narrow view of life, which leaves out the whole of that aspect of life; all receptivity, all gratitude, all inheritance, all worship.[2]

Imagine someone in 1933 reminding us that we did not make ourselves!

[2] G. K. Chesterton, "Our Birthday", *The Chesterton Review*, 10 (November, 1984), 366.

Easter reminds us that we did not make ourselves and, likewise, that we do not save ourselves either. And this is really the best thing about this wonderful feast. For if we did save ourselves, we would have conjured up a very paltry future, probably in this world, probably something like what we already know, rather than something utterly more glorious which we are in fact promised. Such a faith of our own, such a work we formed by ourselves, would be a very narrow doctrine, yielding a quite repulsive little universe. I prefer the idea that at the end of the world, it is already tomorrow in Australia; that there is another manner to our existence; that gratitude, receptivity, and worship are elicited from us in the world that already is. For, in the end, as our Creed teaches us, it is in this world we are called to resurrection and glory, no other.

52

The Pure and Cold Air That Befits
All-Hallows' Day

As I try to reread T. S. Eliot's "Ash Wednesday" on Ash Wednesday (a practice I heartily recommend to all those who doubt our greatness), so I also try to meditate on Belloc's *The Four Men*[1] during those most Christian of days at the end of October and the beginning of November. I have always felt that these days, more than any others, were designed for us, saints and sinners that we are. No Mass is more beautiful than that of All Saints' Day on November 1, and at no time do we remember those of us who have died more than on All Souls' Day on November 2.

These are the days when those of us who are Christian doggedly insist before that world in which there is no hope that we do not believe in God as some sort of abstraction. We insist that we can prove he exists. He is revealed, however, as Someone with whom we shall dwell. No other God is really worth believing in.

Yet the very fact of All Saints' Day and All Souls' Day is a reminder of the risk God took in creating us. Some of us will somehow love him, others of us, probably most of us, will barely succeed in finding him. No doubt it is possible some of us will not choose him at all. If All Saints' Day and All Souls' Day remind us that we can have the glory even of ourselves

[1] Hilaire Belloc, *The Four Men: A Farago* (Oxford: Oxford University Press, 1984).

only if we *choose* it. The Eve of All Hallows' reminds us that
we need not choose it. There are indeed demons and specters
vying for our attention.

Several years ago, a friend of mine spent a semester in England, a friend who believes in giving gifts mindful of place and
time. This is how I happen to own a copy of Belloc's *The Four
Men*, one of the most wondrous books I know. All four men
are, no doubt, Belloc himself, even though each has a name in
the dialogues of the walk that they take together in Sussex.
They are introduced as Grizzlebeard, the Poet, the Sailor, and
"Myself". The walk occurred on those enormously symbolic
Christian days, from October 29 to November 2, in the year
1902; from the days immediately before All-Hallows' Eve, to
All-Hallows' Day, to All Souls' Day.

As the four days ended and the four men were about to part
to their own ways, they decided to have a farewell feast, to cel-
ebrate, as men should, their chance days together. On the 29th
of October, Belloc had found himself drinking port before a
fire in the "George" pub in Robertsbridge, with thoughts
"through which at last came floating a vision of the woods of
home and of another place—the lake where the Arun rises".
So musing, Belloc was determined to see his native country
again, on foot, as only things we love should be seen. The
passingness of things is most poignant at the end of October,
the days grow much shorter, especially in England. You have
crossed land and sea, going about many different duties, "but
all the while your life runs past you like a river, and the things
that are of moment to men you do not know at all"—these are
the words that are difficult to forget: "the things that are of
moment to men". We can pass through our lives and forget to
deal with the things that are important. Is there a sadness
greater than this?

As Belloc thinks these things over, he hit the table with his
fist to emphasize his determination. "As I said these things to
myself I felt as that man felt of whom everybody has read in
Homer with an answering heart: that 'he longed as he jour-
neyed to see once more the smoke going up from his own

land, and after that to die'." Grizzlebeard is unexpectedly in the inn listening to Belloc mutter these things to himself. Grizzlebeard suggests that they set out together. So Belloc accepts the companionship of Grizzlebeard, of his old age, "for all companionship is good, but chance companionship is the best of all".

On the way, the Sailor and the Poet join the walk to discover the smoke going up from Belloc's own land. Belloc did not believe that we loved God apart from real flesh and real blood, apart from our love of bacon and eggs and the sea and the walks along the river Arun that formed his heritage. But I started off with the feast at the end of the walk.

> As thus we decided upon the nature of the feast, the last of the light, long declined, had faded on the horizon behind the latticework of bare branches. The air was pure and cold, as befitted All Hallows', and the far edges of the Downs toward the Hampshire border had level lines of light above them, deeply coloured, full of departure and of rest.[2]

The pure and cold air befits All Hallows' when we see the light above the Downs, light full of departure and rest.

In their discussion about the farewell feast, they had spoken of cheeses and of port. Belloc then speaks to the Poet:

> And undoubtedly, Poet, you acquired in other countries a habit of eating that Gorgonzola cheese, which is made of soap in Connecticut; and Stilton, which is not made at Stilton; and Camembert, and other outlandish things. But in Sussex, let me tell you, we have but one cheese, the name of which is CHEESE. . . . In colour it is yellow, which is the right colour of Cheese. It is neither young nor old. Its taste is that of Cheese, and nothing more. A man may live upon it all the days of his life.[3]

In our own land, where the smoke is seen on the hills, we eat what is best, what is there, the cheese upon which a man may live for the rest of his life.

[2] Ibid., 146.
[3] Ibid., 145–46.

The four men finally find an old inn "brilliantly lighted". There were farmers in for a sale. The four men heard singing from within. They knocked and were let into the inn. They found a pleasant bar with a large room in which fifteen or twenty men were drinking and singing. All were hearty and some old. These men had finished their meal, but the four men ordered theirs,

> which was of such excellence in the way of eggs and bacon, as we had none of us until that morning thought possible upon this side of the grave. The cheese also, of which I have spoken, was put before us, and the new cottage loaves, so that this feast, unlike any other feast that yet was since the beginning of the world, exactly answered to all that the heart had expected of it, and we were contented and were filled.[4]

The four then called for their pipes and drink, Belloc for his black currant port (not that Portuguese concoction that is "but elderberry liquorice and boiled wine"), Grizzlebeard for brandy, the Poet, at "the Sailor's expense", for beer, and the Sailor for claret.

On the following day they took their leave of each other. Grizzlebeard turned to Belloc with "a dreadful solemnity":

> There is nothing at all that remains: nor any house; nor any castle, however strong; nor any love, however tender and sound; nor any comradeship among men, however hardy. Nothing remains but the things of which I will not speak, because we have spoken enough of them already during these four days. But I who am old will give you advice, which is this—to consider chiefly from now onward those permanent things which are, as it were, the shores of this age and the harbours of our glittering and pleasant but dangerous and wholly changeful sea.[5]

With this the four men parted.

As Belloc walked slowly away he was sober. "I went till suddenly I remembered with the pang that catches men at the

[4] Ibid., 147.
[5] Ibid., 157–58.

clang of bells what this time was in November; it was the Day of the Dead." He remembered the earthly immortality of a man who has loved his life and his land.

> Ah! but if a man is part of and rooted in one steadfast piece of earth, which has nourished him and given him his being, and if he can on his side lend it glory and do it service (I thought), it will be a friend to him for ever, and he has outflanked Death in a way.[6]

In the end, Belloc sang his poem about the outflanking of death: "He does not die (I wrote) that can bequeath / Some influence to the land he knows . . ." These are the things that are of moment to men, the pure and cold air that befits All Hallows', the cheese on which a man may live all the days of his life, the feast that was unlike any other that yet was since the beginning of the world, the things that answer to all that the heart expected, the gifts of particular time and place.

It was on All Souls' Day, 1902, that Belloc "full of these thoughts" walked "through the gathering darkness southward across the Downs to my home".

[6] Ibid., 161.

53

On St. Augustine's
"Late, Late Have I Loved Thee"

Book VIII, Chapter 7 of the *Confessions* of St. Augustine is entitled, marvelously: "He Deplores His Wretchedness, That Having Been Born Thirty-Two Years, He Had Not Yet Found Out the Truth" (Oates Edition). In a culture whose public doctrine, oftentimes even ecclesiastical, is theoretical "pluralism"—that is, that there is no "truth" but one's own private feelings—the utter seriousness of Augustine's lament seems, well, silly, doesn't it?

Yet, our society is filled with many bright young men and women, not far from Augustine's then age of thirty-two—I have met some of them—who now know they are but victims of this intellectually relativistic climate which insists on seeing truth as "absolutism", doubt as "truth", and "freedom" as what the culture (or 'the faith') "will" come to believe. Augustine was right, however, when he, who had lived through all the alternatives in a way perhaps no one else ever had, described the resultant condition of unlimited freedom and doubt as "wretchedness".

The late Senator John East wrote an essay[1] in which he suggested that a study of Augustine, not Aquinas, was the real intellectual need of our time, especially in international relations, if we are accurately to describe and understand just what

[1] John East, "The Political Relevance of St. Augustine", *Modern Age*, 16 (Spring 1972), 167–81.

it is men "do" to each other. Who, after all, can explain official and non-official terrorism but Augustine?

Although I hold that perhaps the greatest "Augustinian" who ever lived was Aquinas himself, I would agree with East that ours is an era for which Augustine's time has come again. I say "again" for, as Christopher Dawson in two penetrating essays, "Saint Augustine and His Age", pointed out, Augustine comes back again and again to those ages which are no longer able to define or perceive what goes on in the human heart.[2] The results eventually force them to turn back to Augustine, who, they find, accurately describes what they experience.

All of this I bring up here because a friend called me up to remind me that 1986 was the 1600th anniversary of the conversion of Saint Augustine. Evidently, there had been a discussion as to the curious fate of the word "confession" in our day.

Formerly, as for Augustine, confession meant a kind of private, often embarrassing, colloquium with God, though one that needed acknowledgment before men because we are bound to one another, even in our evils. But the notion of confession today almost seems to be an exaltation of one's self, no matter what that self might have been responsible for, a sign of an odd uniqueness, however achieved. The classical tradition, however, suggested that ultimately, some kinds of fame we do not want. Some things are to be confessed only in sorrow.

All of this reminded me of a lecture I once heard Frank Sheed give at Catholic University. Sheed, to recall, had published a fine translation of the *Confessions*. One day, it seems, he was walking down some main street, in London or New York, I forget which, and saw, across the street, a huge sign in a bookstore window, blaring that this book on sale was "Sex-Charged". "Well, naturally", Sheed continued with some amusement, "I walked across the street to see what this book

[2] Christopher Dawson, "St. Augustine and His Age", in *Augustine*, edited by M. C. D'Arcy (New York: Meridian, 1969), 11–78.

might be; and lo, it turned out to be my translation of Augustine's *Confessions*!"

And Augustine, I suppose, does have, for our "experience"-oriented times, a certain polemical advantage over Aquinas, whose most famous and only exploit in these areas seems to have been, with a red-hot poker, to drive a lady hired by his brothers out of the castle, so he could go back to Aristotle and the Dominicans. In any case, both Augustine and Aquinas would have agreed that there were things about us concerning which we would just as soon not have anybody know but God and this only because we know he is merciful.

"And I spoke many things loudly and earnestly, in the *sorrow of my remembrance*," Augustine wrote in Book IX, in an unforgettable passage.

The last chapter of the *Confessions* begins, "We therefore see those things which Thou madest, because they are; but they are because Thou seest them." It is all there, isn't it?

Probably the most famous lines of Augustine—"Late, late have I loved Thee"—were written by a man unwilling to content himself with not seeing, by a man who knew he did not, at thirty-two, know the truth, but who also knew that this truth existed to be seen, to be remembered, and that his life (and all life) would be meaningless if based on the idea that there was no truth.

Augustine is a man also for our time, even 1600 years after his conversion. He had already lived through all the lives which our culture proposes as "possible". Augustine learned personally that many sorts of life were "possible", but he also remembered that their very possibility left his heart restless. We are an age, I suspect, in which this theoretic "restlessness" is so pervasive that we cannot escape from it even in religion.

And from Book X, let me conclude:

> This is the fruit of my confessions, not of what I was, but of what I am, that I may confess this not before Thee only, in a secret exaltation with trembling, and a secret sorrow with hope, but in the ears also of the believing sons of men—partakers of my joy, and sharers of my mortality, my fellow-

citizens and the companions of my pilgrimage, those who are gone before, and those that are to follow after. . . .

We are those who now "follow after". For us, the *Confessions*, after 1600 years, remains the beginning book somewhere about the time we reach thirty-two, when we also can speak, with Augustine, because we now notice that things exist because God sees them first, because we now understand "the sorrow of my remembrance".

54

On Being Sought

"In Christianity, however, the human soul is not the seeker but the sought", C. S. Lewis wrote in his *Studies in Medieval and Renaissance Literature*. "It is God who seeks, who descends from the other world to find and heal man." In Plato, for example, the philosopher is pictured as someone who is drawn, attracted by the Good which calls him outside of himself by being what it is. In a sense, both of these views can be true, but the former one implies that God is active on our part and in our world.

Sometimes, however, we have a picture of the world in which each of us works out the drama of his particular experience as if he were doing God a favor by seeking him out—whoever "he" might be. Since we think the center of existence is ourselves, we suspect the world should be quite grateful if we let any of its alien elements into the closed circle of our own self-definition. We think we do God a sort of favor by wondering whether he exists or whether he loves us.

Introspection, as it is called, looking into ourselves, can often deceive us into discovering in ourselves only ourselves. I have always found this to be a rather unsettling prospect. The very last thing I want to discover about the world is that it is largely composed of and by myself.

But early on, I had read Aristotle, who told me that I could not even know myself if I did not know something else. Too, I had read Saint Augustine, who explained to us in his

Confessions, that when we look into the depths even of ourselves, we do not find only ourselves.

Thus I believe that great men and great books can save us in a way, if we are to be saved, even though it is not "men" who save us. I put little trust in collectivities, and I would not prefer one to a single human person. Our redemption—we must be found *and* healed, as both Lewis and Augustine said—can only be a "self-redemption" if the Incarnation took place. And even then, it is ours only if we choose it, given the grace to do so.

Humility, that virtue which enables us to be content with being somewhat less than the angels, advises us not to take ourselves so seriously that we must think that we "cause" all else to be. We are to allow *what is* to teach us. We misunderstand the virtue of humility, Chesterton said, if we locate it in the intellect and not in our will, if we use it to doubt our capacity to know anything instead of our capacity to do the right thing by ourselves alone.

What happens to us, then, if we picture the world and all in it, especially others like ourselves, *not* as a locus in which we seek truth and goodness and reality, but where truth and goodness and *the reality that is* seek us? The first thing that happens, I think, is that we "dis-establish", as it were, the intellectual from the center of reality on such a hypothesis. The intellectual—or anyone, for that matter, since the intellectual does not have a monopoly on rejecting *what is*—is thus moved from the center of reality.

We are always not a little perturbed that publicans and harlots will enter the Kingdom before the scribes and the pharisees of every age. This seems "unjust" and perhaps it is, since it is not "justice" but "mercy" that rules the foundations of the world, as Saint Thomas said. Whatever it is that seeks each of us out in our very particularities, it is not like a sort of 5–4 Court decision that went our way.

Yvor Winters once wrote a poem called, appropriately, "To William Dinsmore Briggs Conducting His Seminar". To me, its concluding lines seem to be a monument to those who only seek, who only reshuffle the world into their own self-defining images:

> And in the godless thin electric glare
> I watched your face spurn momently along
> Till the dark moments close and wrinkles verge
> On the definitive and final stare:
> And that hard book will now contain this wrong.[1]

The perils of redirecting the chosen, "made" world back into possibility and probability are very much alive inside of each of us, especially those who pretend a certain excellence, a certain intelligence, a certain culture.

What is the alternative? To cease thinking? Hardly. Christianity is, above all, a religion of accurate thinking. It is a religion in which definitions count because the mind is a faculty for making them, in which "this is not that", in which the *Word* was made flesh, and not air. Perhaps nothing today is more agonizing than the sloppiness of so much Christian thinking in which ideology passes for dogma.

Yet it remains true: Even though we have intellects, given as parts of ourselves, to do what intellects do, to say *what is*, still our thought alone will not save us. Indeed, our thought will not long remain even thought unless we are open to the idea that we are first sought, first loved, first in need of being healed.

An old *Peanuts* showed Marcie going out the door by a forlorn Peppermint Patty: "I can't walk to school with you any more, Sir. I'm on Patrol Duty. . . . I have to get to my post." Peppermint Patty, pondering the duty-versus-love theme by herself, sighs, "What are friends for if you can't forget them?"

The structure of the world is such that none of us is a forgotten being. We are creatures who, in being sought, can seek, even in our rambles and idylls, even in where we are. When we know this, we know why we can have such a thing as a spiritual life, we who are the mortals.

---

[1] Yvor Winters, *Collected Poems* (Athens, OH: Swallow, 1952), 47.

CONCLUSION

"A STEADY AND RECIPROCAL ATTACHMENT"

The most important words in stories are "Once upon a time . . .", or "And so they lived happily ever after." In our essays, in our "lighter" essays, as I have called them, in those essays that reflect our faith and, yes, our foolishness, our good sense and our oddities, we realize that we each have our own "once upon a time" and we are each unsettled by the thought that, in some sense, the "happiness ever after" is also in our own hands, even though it seems ultimately to be a gift to us.

The last words of *The Pickwick Papers* are these:

> Every year, he [Mr. Pickwick] repairs to a large family merry-making at Mr. Wardle's; on this, as on all other occasions, he is invariably attended by the faithful Sam, between whom and his master there exists a steady and reciprocal attachment which nothing but death will terminate.[1]

We wonder about this conclusion, don't we, whether such termination will negate the "happiness ever after"? The "steady and reciprocal attachment" seems almost to be the most important thing about us, that is, the abiding status of our friends and loves given to us in this world.

Belloc, in *The Four Men*, I was reminded, addressed himself to this feeling, to this perplexity that we must each experience if we want to write essays at all, if we want to make sense even of the most contented of human lives like that of Mr. Pickwick. Chesterton, as he told us in his biography of Dickens,

---

[1]Charles Dickens, *The Pickwick Papers* (New York: Washington Square, 1960), 860.

expected to meet Mr. Pickwick drinking great flagons at "The Inn at the End of the World". I have always loved that particular Inn.

On October 30, 1902, Belloc listened to Grizzlebeard who, addressing us all, spoke most solemnly in this manner:

> Everything else that there is in the action of the mind save loving is of its nature a growth; it goes through its phases of seed, of miraculous sprouting, of maturity, and somnolescence, and of decline. But with loving it is not so; for the comprehension by one soul of another is something borrowed from whatever lies outside time: it is not under the conditions of time.[2]

Not under the condition of time—time out of time—our idylls and rambles belong primarily to such time, I think, particularly as we live them, as we seek to write about them so that we can again seek the inner meaning that we may have missed in their living. For it does seem true, our actions need words as much as our words proceed to action and, in turn, are reflections and illuminations on them.

In *The Rambler* for October 1, 1751, Samuel Johnson told of finding a new, less ostentatious place to live. "When I first cheapened my lodgings", he wrote,

> the landlady told me, that she hoped I was not an author, for the lodgers on the first floor had stipulated that the upper rooms should not be occupied by a noisy trade.[3]

He assured the landlady that his own particular "trade" would not disturb the lodgers. Yet we cannot help but realize that some things do unsettle us, disturb us. And certainly the trade of writing and reading essays occupies us and takes us out of our world, a world too much surrounded by "stipulations" that prevent us from seeing *what is*.

As I remarked in the beginning, fifty-four essays are found in this collection because that was the number chosen to appear

[2] Hilaire Belloc, *The Four Men: A Farago* (Oxford: Oxford University Press, 1984), 27.

[3] Samuel Johnson, *Rasselas, Poems, and Selected Prose*, ed. Bertrand H. Bronson (New York: Holt, 1958), 121.

in Belloc's *Selected Essays*. In fifty-four essays, we can cover much ground, from Rome to Waltham Abbey, to the church in Pocahontas where I was baptized, to Washington in the Spring, and to Clement Street in San Francisco.

Even names and titles, like "The Turning Point Inn" or Chesterton's "Inn at the End of the World", seem to epitomize our lot. Place reminds us that we are earth-bound creatures and that this too is our glory. And time, time-out-of-time, the "*nunc stans*", as Saint Thomas called it, the *now* that *stands*, remains, to remind us of the instant that does not seem to pass at all. "A steady and reciprocal attachment" is rather what we seek even in this world.

"The comprehension by one soul of another is something borrowed from whatever lies outside time", as Belloc mused. Somehow, as I have tried to explain, I have always thought that the short, lightsome essay is the best way to remind us that our pathway to the beyondness of time begins and remains in the particular days, in the common and extraordinary places we can describe in much detail because we were once there.

Ordinary, chaotic days can have perfect endings, and we are a finite lot. If I conclude by maintaining, as I do maintain, that our lives are a steady, often delightful, sometimes sad, series of idylls and rambles, the reader no longer will be surprised. And yet he will be surprised. The capacity to be surprised comes close to the very definition of our dignity.

"No one could imagine that these essays could have been written by another hand", J. B. Morton said of Belloc. And yet, I trust, that on reading these essays, anyone can now at last begin to imagine the world written by this hand. Let me cite one last time from *The Rambler*, from Saturday, March 14, 1751, the last issue of that remarkable journal. "Time, which puts an end to all human pleasures and sorrows, has likewise concluded the labours of *The Rambler*", Johnson wrote.

But because he wrote precisely an essay, Johnson's rambles did not end. I must confess to finding in that realization a kind of gladness, not sorrow, a genuine human pleasure that someone from down the ages left such wonderful lines for me to read, even yet. These "lighter Christian essays", as I have presumed to call them, are what I have to leave. They could not, I think, have been "written by another hand".